HR L OO A

A color guide to familiar

FLOWERING SHRUBS

A color guide to familiar
FLOWERING
SHRUBS

By J. Pokorný   .

Illustrated by J. Kaplická

OCTOPUS BOOKS

Translated by Olga Kuthanová
Graphic design: Soňa Valoušková

English version first published 1975 by
OCTOPUS BOOKS LIMITED
59 Grosvenor Street, London W1

© 1974 Artia, Prague

ISBN 0 7064 0346 0

Distributed in Australia by
Rigby Limited
30 North Terrace, Kent Town
Adelaide, South Australia 5067

Printed in Czechoslovakia

3/10/07/51

CONTENTS

FOREWORD

This book is intended to provide nature lovers with a better knowledge of the shrubs they may come across in the countryside as well as in the city. It contains 64 colour plates showing a flowering or fruiting twig of each shrub with the leaves, fruit and seed. A twig with winter buds is also shown to aid identification of the shrub even during its dormant period. The brief text accompanying each plate describes the morphological features and calls attention to the specific distinguishing features. Included in this book are common shrubs growing in the wild in western and central Europe, including Great Britain, as well as a number of shrubs that have become established in Europe through long cultivation and are commonly used in landscaping. Stated in each case is roughly the area of the shrub's distribution and the characteristics of the locality where it is to be found. There are also notes on the species' requirements as regards light, soil, moisture and fertility, and in some instances also their hardiness.

Since shrubs, like trees, brighten housing estates and parks as well as private gardens with their green foliage and a great many nature lovers are actively engaged in gardening, the introductory chapters as well as the text accompanying the individual colour plates give instructions relating to their propagation, cultivation and care.

The shrubs in this book are arranged botanically with both the Latin and common English name of each species; also included in parentheses are common synonyms. More detailed information about the nourishment of trees and shrubs, the structure of the trunk, crown, roots and other plant parts will be found in the preceding book of this series, 'Trees'. The following pages acquaint the reader only with the principal morphological features and explain the terminology used in the text.

SHRUBS AND THEIR IMPORTANCE

Shrubs are closely related to trees, the two supplementing each other in complex forest communities where the former form the lower layer. Their shorter height and better adaptability to extreme conditions enable them to penetrate even areas where trees cannot grow and to establish extensive thickets. One example is the high mountain shrub community above the tree line consisting of dwarf pine, European green alder, dwarf willows, rhododendrons and other shrubs whose limited height coupled with a protective blanket of snow permits them to survive the icy winds and sub-zero temperatures of the winter months. Beyond the Arctic Circle, in regions with a shallow layer of soil that thaws only during the brief summer season, the shrub communities include arctic species such as dwarf willows and birches. Similar species grow on peaty soils in the mountains and foothills. In dry plains areas we also find shrub communities, but composed of different species adapted to their environment.

The main characteristics that differentiate the shrub from the tree are the structure of the trunk and the height it attains. Unlike trees, shrubs generally have more than a single stem, branching close to the ground to form several thinner stems that grow to a maximum of 5—8 m in height. These general criteria, however, do not always apply. Some species of shrubs may include specimens with a clearly evident main stem (Cornelian cherry, common buckthorn, English holly), and in rare instances some may even attain a height of more than 8 m (hawthorn, English holly). These general characteristics, however, apply to the majority of shrubs.

Shrubs may be divided according to their height into the following groups: a) tall shrubs (3—8 m high) such as hazel, hawthorn, sea buckthorn, b) medium-size shrubs (1—3 m high), this being the largest group, and c) low shrubs (up to 1 m high) such as mezereon. Of importance from the gardening standpoint is the division of shrubs into evergreen species (English holly, mahonia, box, etc.) and deciduous species (most central European shrubs). Important in park landscaping are climbing and rambling shrubs (common ivy, traveller's joy, honeysuckle) for walls, fences, arbours, pergolas and pillars. Shrubs may be further divided according to various criteria, e.g. fast-growing and slow-growing, thorny and non-thorny, but these distinctions are of lesser significance.

Shrubs have aesthetic value in the landscape, particularly in parks and gardens. The heart of every nature lover gladdens in spring at the sight of a rocky hillside with here and there the white flowers of blackthorn and hawthorn or the yellow blooms of the cornelian cherry. Just as lovely are the pink blossoms of dog rose scattered in the pastures or the yellow patches of common broom on heaths and at the edges of forests. Shrubs growing in woodlands or at the margins of forests are not so easily pollinated by the wind as their taller companions the trees and for that reason they are generally adapted for pollination by insects, hence their bright flowers. At the first hint of spring the sallow provides bees with their first nourishment of pollen and nectar after their long winter sleep. In March sun-warmed hillsides in central and eastern Europe are covered with the yellow blooms of the cornelian cherry, which likewise attract swarms of bees. And with the actual arrival of spring, there is a wealth of blossom in shades of yellow, pink, red and other hues, as shrubs in hedgerows, pastures and forest clearings entice their many and varied insect pollinators. The fruits and seeds of shrubs are disseminated, as a rule, by birds and animals that eat the sweet pulp or protein-rich and oily seeds. The fruits of the common elder, red elder, currants, privet, English holly, blackthorn and many other shrubs are favourites with birds and their seeds are dispersed far and wide. For songbirds, however, shrubs are not just a source of food. The dense and sometimes thorny branches of many shrubs provide them with shelter. Countless nests may be found in thickets growing on the perimeters of fields, pastures, by the wayside and at the edges of woods, and the densely growing branches also afford protection against birds and beasts of prey.

Small game (partridge, pheasant, hare and rabbit) likewise find thickets and hedgerows good protection against predators and shelter in inclement weather. That is the reason we should seek to preserve solitary shrubs as well as groups of shrubs growing on field boundaries, by the wayside, at the margins of forests and abandoned quarries as well as other barren places. Not only are they decorative but also an important habitat of many birds and animals.

Even more important are the shrubs growing in parks and gardens. Shrubs which are undergrowth species make it possible to divide a park into many sections and secluded areas. A belt of shrubs can serve to separate a children's playground from a frequented path or other section of the park and thus create a separate children's realm. A semi-circle of shrubs around a few benches will make such a spot into an island where one can pass a pleasant hour with a book or in quiet conversation without being disturbed. A belt of shrubs planted on the park's periphery separates it from the bustling activity of city streets and serves the purpose far better than a wall or fence. And then there is the element of colour. How dull parks and gardens would be without the bright patches of flowering rhododendron, jasmine, spiraea, quince, hydrangea and other shrubs! Flowering shrubs are an ornament in any garden and a suitable selection of various species makes it possible to have a continuity of colour the whole year through where mild winters prevail. Flowering shrubs are in many cases an excellent substitute for flower beds, which often require much time and effort, besides being costly to maintain. In every park, garden and housing estate there should be at least as many shrubs as there are trees. Parks with few shrubs are testimony to neglect and lack of care on the part of park attendants. Evergreen shrubs are also an important element in landscape architecture. Not only do they brighten parks and gardens in winter when deciduous trees and shrubs are bare but they also serve as a green undergrowth in groves of trees where turf is hard to maintain for lack of light. The flora of western and central Europe comprises few such native evergreen species and so it is necessary to augment these with certain shrubs of Asian or American origin. Besides the European genera (*Buxus, Ilex, Hedera, Ruscus,* etc.) the evergreens include primarily members of the genus *Berberis, Cotoneaster, Euonymus, Kalmia, Mahonia, Laurocerasus, Pyracantha* and *Viburnum.*

Climbing and scrambling shrubs are valuable assets that have few substitutes. Ideal for covering and concealing ugly walls and fences as well as for adding a touch of green to terraces, pergolas, archways and pillars are members of the genera *Ampelopsis, Aristolochia, Clematis, Euonymus, Hedera, Hydrangea, Lonicera, Rosa, Vitis* and many others.

The loveliest features of parks as well as private gardens and often also true masterpieces of the gardener's art are heath and rock gardens. Here, in particular, shrubs and sub- or semi-shrubs play an important role. Heath gardens are made up almost exclusively of shrubs and sub-shrubs, the most common being *Vaccinium, Pernettya, Rhododendron, Kalmia, Ledum, Erica* and *Calluna.* Best suited for rock gardens, apart from certain dwarf evergreens, are various members of the genera *Cotoneaster, Cytisus, Daphne, Erica, Vaccinium, Berberis, Rhododendron, Hebe,* etc.

Some deciduous shrubs are often used to form hedges of varying height and thickness because they stand up well to pruning. These include also certain thorny species that form practically impenetrable hedges. For this purpose, shrubs may be divided into two groups: those that form hedges more than 2 m high and those that grow to a height of 1—1.5 m. The first group includes *Caragana arborescens, Chaenomeles lagenaria, Crataegus laevigata (oxyacantha), Ligustrum vulgare, Lonicera tatarica, Physocarpus opulifolius* and *Syringa vulgaris;* the second *Berberis thunbergii, Buxus sempervirens, Mahonia aquifolium, Prunus spinosa, Ribes alpinum, Rosa rugosa* and *Spiraea × vanhouttei.*

Besides their importance in landscaping, shrubs also yield raw materials for industrial use. Despite their small dimensions the wood of certain shrubs is much in demand either because of its excellent properties or for special uses (cornelian cherry, box, alder buckthorn, spindle tree, etc.). The wood, bark and leaves of other shrubs yield products needed by the rubber and leather industries (spindle tree, smoke tree, staghorn sumach, etc.). Many shrubs have healing properties and their flowers, fruits, leaves or bark are collected for pharmaceutical purposes (hawthorn, elder, alder buckthorn, common buckthorn, etc.). Quite a few bear fruits rich in vitamins or of great nutrient value and these are processed by the food industry (hazel, blackthorn, quince, raspberry, dog rose, cornelian cherry, etc.). The foregoing is naturally only a brief list, for in many regions certain shrubs and their parts are used for still other purposes and in the making of a great variety of products.

THE ORGANS AND PARTS OF A SHRUB

Leaves

The leaves of plants are very important. They are the plant's manufacturing organs and act also in the capacity of lungs and partly as an excretory system. The most important plant function takes place in the leaves. Called photosynthesis, it is a process whereby the chlorophyll in the leaf cells with the aid of the sun's energy transforms atmospheric carbon dioxide into organic substances essential to plant growth.

The plant, like all living organisms, also breathes, i.e. it absorbs oxygen and exhales carbon dioxide. This, too, takes place mainly in the leaves. The leaves likewise serve as an organ of transpiration, excess water absorbed by the roots being passed back to the atmosphere from the leaf surface in the form of vapour after the plant has extracted the mineral substances contained therein.

The proportion of carbon dioxide in the air is very low and the plant must therefore process great quantities of air and absorption must thus take place on the greatest possible leaf surface. That is why plant leaves are so thin and why a mature shrub has several hundreds to thousands of leaves. The placing of the leaves in the crown likewise contributes to the better utilization of light. This is aided by the intricate branching of the crown as well as by the varying length and angle of the leaf stalks. Respiration and transpiration take place through pores or stomata. These are microscopic openings in the epidermis of the leaf, located, as a rule, on the underside. They can be expanded or contracted to control the evaporation of water, depending on whether there is an overabundance or lack of this vital substance. Water is transported to the leaves via a vein-like system of vascular bundles that pass through the leaf stalk and branch in the leaf blade into an elaborate pattern.

Though all leaves have the same function, those of the various species differ in shape, thus serving as an important means of identification. Distinguishing features of the leaf are the overall shape, the margin, the arrangement on the twig, the venation (vein pattern), and in some cases also the hairiness of the surface. According to their arrangement leaves are either alternate, where only a single leaf is attached at each node on the twig and the leaves are usually arranged in spirals, as in the

Fig. 1. Leaf shapes: Simple leaves: 1) hazel, 2) white currant. Compound leaves: 3) trifoliate (golden rain), 4) palmately compound *(Caragana frutex)*, 5) odd-pinate (bladder senna), 6) even-pinnate (pea tree).

hazel, hawthorn and barberry, or opposite, with leaves paired at the same point, one on each side of the twig, e.g. the dogwood, spindle tree, lilac and ash.

Leaves may be either simple, with a single blade, which may be lobed, e.g. the hazel, gooseberry and hawthorn, or compound, with three or more blades attached to one stalk, e.g. the bladdernut and common elder. Simple leaves have blades of various shapes and are described accordingly as acicular, lanceolate, ovate, obovate, orbicular, cordate, rhomboid, etc. Compound leaves may be trifoliate, palmately compound, odd-pinnate or even-pinnate. Trifoliate has three leaflets radiating from the end of the rachis, e.g. the laburnum and common broom. Palmately compound has more than three leaflets radiating from the end of the rachis, e.g. *Rubus fruticosus*. Odd-pinnate has pairs of leaflets attached laterally on the rachis and a single one at the tip as in the case of the rose, bladdernut and common elder. Even-pinnate has an even number of leaflets attached laterally on the rachis in pairs, as in the case of the pea tree.

Leaf margins are smooth and entire (e.g. the common cotoneaster, woodbine, cornelian cherry and dogwood), serrate (the common elder, blackthorn and rose), double serrate (the hazel, European green alder and raspberry), toothed (the English holly and mahonia) or lobed (the hawthorn and currant).

The leaf blade is patterned with veins. The leaves of most woody plants have one principal vein with several branching veins extending to the leaf margin. Some perennial plants, usually those with palmately lobed leaves, have palmate venation with several veins of like thickness radiating from the end of the rachis (e.g. gooseberry). A good identifying feature of some shrubs is their arcuate venation (cornelian cherry, dogwood, common buckthorn), where the secondary veins run parallel to the leaf margin towards the tip of the leaf.

Leaf apices likewise differ in shape; they may be acuminate or acute (with long, slender, or short points), rounded, truncate (blunt) or emarginate (cleft). Leaf bases may be rounded (European green alder, wayfaring tree), cuneate, i.e. wedge-shaped, (barberry, mezereon) or cordate (hazel).

Most shrubs native to central and western Europe are deciduous, that is to say they shed their leaves in winter. With the onset of autumn the organic substances in the leaves are concentrated in the plant stem and roots and the leaves begin to change colour. This is caused by the decomposition of the green chlorophyll, the predominance of yellow xanthophyll and red carotenoid pigments and increased level of anthocyanin in the cell plasm. Autumn coloration is likewise a distinguishing feature in a number of shrubs. Thus, for instance, the leaves of *Cornus mas*, *Euonymus europaeus*, *Rhus typhina* and *Berberis thunbergi*

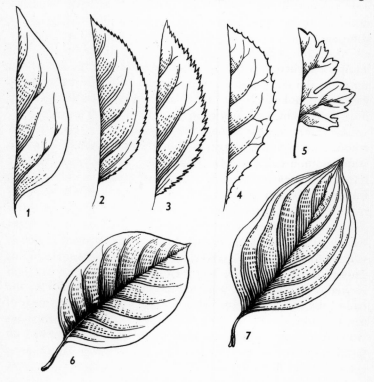

Fig. 2. Leaf margins: 1) entire, 2) serrate, 3) doubly-serrate, 4) toothed, 5) lobed.
Venation: 6) pinnate, 7) arcuate.

turn purplish-red, those of *Forsythia suspensa* dark violet, *Viburnum opulus* scarlet, *Amelanchier ovalis* orange, *Rhamnus frangula* and *Corylus avellana* yellow, etc. These autumn hues make just as lovely a picture in parks and in the wild as do the pastel tints of flowering shrubs in spring.

Later a corky layer forms between the stalk and the twig, severing the vascular bundles nourishing the leaf. The leaf then falls to the ground, leaving a pale spot on the twig which is called the leaf scar. In some cases this scar has a characteristic shape and helps in identifying the species in the winter months.

Flowers

Flowers are the plant's organs of propagation, giving rise to a new individual by sexual reproduction, namely the fusion of the male gamete (pollen grain) and female gamete (ovule). The flowers of seed plants are actually leaves modified for reproduction. In the full-petalled flower it is possible to distinguish four different sets of modified leaves: the calyx, corolla, stamens (male sexual organs) and pistil (female sexual organ). The flowers of most shrubs have all four parts; in some species, however, (e.g. the hazel and European green alder) the calyx and corolla may be absent, as is often the case in trees. Shrubs growing beneath trees have very poor chances of being pollinated by the wind and are usually pollinated by insects. Their flowers therefore often have bright colours and strong fragrance in order to attract insects. For their services — visiting different flowers and transferring pollen from one to another — they are rewarded with the nectar that we, too, enjoy in the form of honey, made in the nests or hives of bees. Many shrubs are important honey-yielding plants and are often cultivated by bee-keepers, e.g. the cornelian cherry, snowberry, raspberry, etc.

A flower is composed of the following parts:

calyx — the external, usually green leafy part

corolla — the inner floral envelope consisting of petals, usually brightly coloured

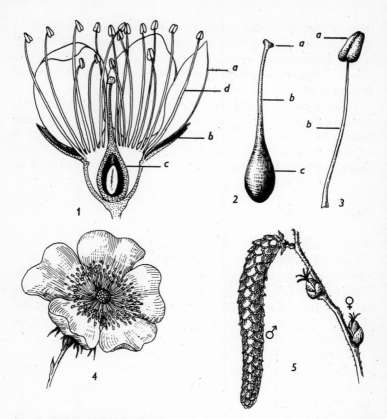

Fig. 3. 1) Diagram of the flower of blackthorn: a — corolla, b — calyx,
c — pistil, d — stamens.
2) Pistil: a — stigma, b — style, c — ovary.
3) Stamen: a — anther, b — filament.
4) Hermaphrodite flower. 5) Unisexual flower (hazel).

stamens — consisting of anthers and filaments; when ripe, the
anthers burst and release the microscopic pollen grains that
look like yellow powder
pistil — the ovule-bearing organ deriving from the fusion of one
or several carpels; it comprises the ovary containing ovules
and a style bearing a sticky or hairy stigma to which the
pollen grains adhere and grow downward to the ovary.

Flowers may be classified according to whether they possess both or only one (or none) of the sexual organs. They are bisexual, having both stamens and pistil (e.g. rose, bladdernut,

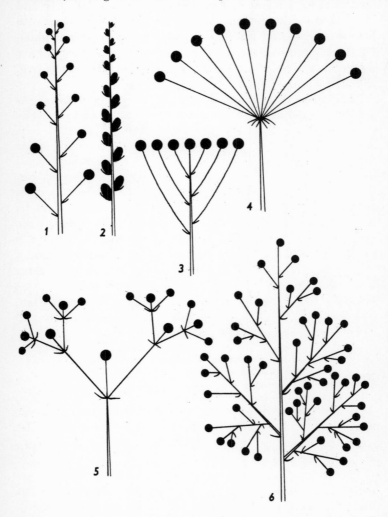

Fig. 4. Types of inflorescence: 1) raceme, 2) spike, 3) panicle, 4) umbel, 5) dichasium, 6) cyme.

cornelian cherry, dogwood), or unisexual, having only the male or female organ or one of the two atrophied (e.g. willow, mistletoe and sea buckthorn). Barren flowers lack functional sexual organs altogether. Examples are the snowball tree and some kinds of hydrangea. Monoecious shrubs are ones with both staminate and pistillate flowers on the same individual, e.g. hazel, green alder, etc., whereas dioecious shrubs have staminate and pistillate flowers on different individuals, e.g. mistletoe, sea buckthorn, willow, etc.

The flowers of trees and shrubs are rarely single blooms. As a rule they are borne in clusters of various shapes and sizes. The commonest types are the spike or catkin, with sessile flowers attached directly to the stalk, e.g. those of the willow, alder and hazel; the raceme, with an elongated axis bearing flowers on short stems blossoming in succession toward the apex, e.g. the barberry, currant and golden rain; the panicle, with a main central stem and branched laterals bearing flowers, e.g. the traveller's joy, spiraea, smoke tree and staghorn sumach; the umbel, in which the axis is very much contracted so that the stalked florets form a flat or domed cluster, e.g. the cornelian cherry and English holly; the cyme, with stems bearing flowers on individual stalks of unequal length so that all are at the same height, e.g. the hawthorn and spiraea; and the dichasium, with two branches of flowers set below the terminal flower and extending beyond it, e.g. the spindle tree.

Fruits and Seeds

After fertilization the ovary ripens into the fruit, its outer layer forming the wall or pericarp with one or more seeds inside. The seed is the fertilized ripened ovule and consists of the embryo and nutritive tissue enclosed in a hard cover.

The fruits of deciduous plants are either true fruits, i.e. merely the ripened ovary, or are accessory fruits, developed from the ovary plus other parts of the flower (stem, petals). Included in the latter group are the pome, the hip, raspberry and blackberry, though these are actually multiple fruits.

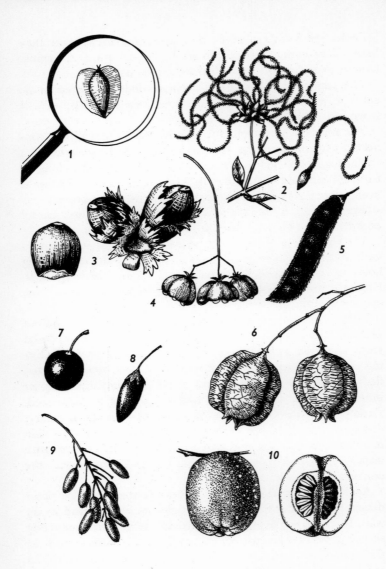

Fig. 5. Fruits of shrubs: a — dry: 1,2) samara (birch, clematis), 3) nut (hazel), 4) capsule (spindle tree), 5) legume (Scotch broom), 6) follicle (bladdernut); b — fleshy: 7) drupe (blackthorn), 8,9) berry (box thorn, barberry), 10) pome (Japanese quince).

Fruits are furthermore divided, according to whether they have a dry or soft pericarp, into dry fruits (samara, nut, legume, follicle, capsule) and fleshy fruits (berries, drupes).

The samara is a dry, usually one-seeded fruit, shed in its entirety, with thin, membranous to leathery pericarp; often it is winged.

The nut is a hard-shelled fruit with a woody wall not connected with the seed, e.g. that of the hazel and smoke tree.

The legume or pod is a one-celled, flattened, usually elongate fruit, splitting along the margins when ripe, with several seeds inside, e.g. the golden rain, pea tree and common broom.

The follicle is a one-celled fruit, developed from one carpel and dehiscing along a single suture, e.g. the spiraea.

The capsule is a single or many-celled fruit splitting in various ways when ripe, e.g. by means of a lid, developing holes or disintegrating irregularly. It contains several seeds. Examples are the bladdernut, spindle tree, mock orange, box, etc.

Fleshy fruits do not split when ripe but drop from the parent plant in their entirety or else break up into parts with enclosed seeds. One such fruit is the drupe, which has a pericarp consisting of three layers, namely the thin epicarp or outer layer, fleshy mesocarp or middle layer and hard bony endocarp or inner layer that is the stone, usually encasing a single seed. Examples are the blackthorn, English holly, cornelian cherry, dogwood, etc. Another fleshy fruit is the berry, with a thin membranous covering and fleshy middle and inner layer with usually several seeds embedded in the pulpy mass, e.g. the currant, privet, common elder.

Accessory fruits include the pome and the hip. The pome develops from the fusion of the fleshy receptacle and ovary wall. It is a fleshy fruit consisting of a central core containing several seeds and an outer thickened fleshy layer. Examples are the cotoneaster, hawthorn, quince, medlar and crab apple. The hip is a multiple fruit consisting of a fleshy hollow receptacle enclosing several achenes.

The fruit contains one, several or many seeds. The seed consists of a membranous or hard covering and inner nucleus.

The nucleus consists of either just the embryo and food reserves for the initial period of growth stored in its cotyledons (or seed leaves) or else embryo plus endosperm (nutritive tissue enclosing the embryo). Clearly discernible on the seeds of some woody plants is the scar called the hilum marking the spot where it was attached to the fruit. This is usually light in colour, e.g. in

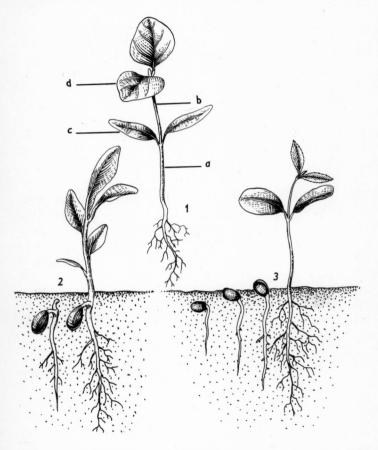

Fig. 6. 1) Seedling features: a — hypocotyl, b — epicotyl, c — cotyledon, d — primary leaves.
2) Hypogeal germination (mezereon).
3) Germination (spindle tree).

Fig. 7. Shrub seedlings: 1)green alder, 2) barberry, 3) mahonia, 4) rose, 5) currant, 6) hawthorn, 7) cotoneaster, 8) blackthorn.

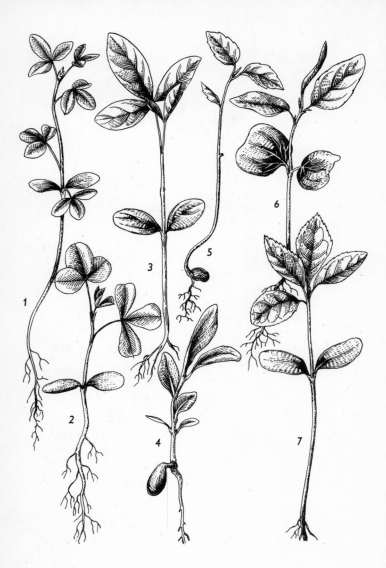

1) common broom, 2) pea tree, 3) golden rain, 4) mezereon, 5) alder buckthorn, 6) common buckthorn, 7) spindle tree.

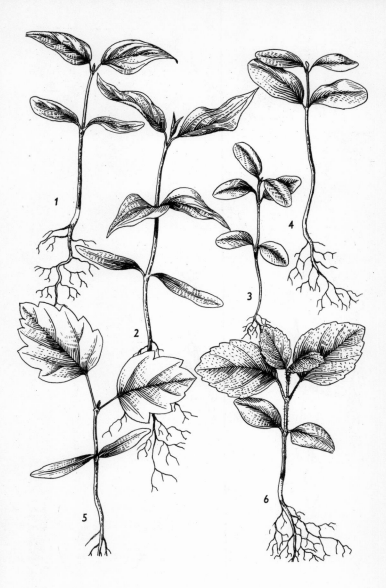

1) dogwood, 2) cornelian cherry, 3) honeysuckle, 4) privet, 5) guelder rose, 6) wayfaring tree.

the bladdernut, golden rain and common broom. It is the spot through which the seed absorbs the greatest amount of water during germination and also through which the sprouts generally grow.

On rupturing the seed coat the first root turns downward due to the pull of gravity, thus anchoring the emerging seedling in the soil. The hypocotyl or first stem then grows up towards the soil surface, where it straightens and pulls up the two green cotyledons. These are an important part of the seedling since they contain food reserves for the initial period of growth and also chlorophyll for making new food by means of photosynthesis. The deciduous shrubs of Europe all have two cotyledons that differ in shape from the true leaves. They are usually fleshy, entire, elliptical or round; sometimes, however, also lanceolate or lobed. In most instances they last only a short while, drying up and being shed after one to three months. The axis of the plant embryo (the epicotyl) continues to grow above the cotyledons and in time produces the first true leaves.

During germination the cotyledons either grow above the ground or remain below the surface, the first instance being termed epigeal and the second hypogeal germination. Hypogeal germination is more common in trees with large seeds; in the case of shrubs mentioned in this book it is found only in *Corylus avellana*, *Rhamnus frangula* and *Daphne mezereum*. All other shrubs are characterized by epigeal germination.

Buds and Twigs

Buds are young undeveloped shoots containing leaves and sometimes flowers. They are an important means of identification in winter when trees and shrubs are leafless.

The terminal bud is located at the tip of a twig or branch and is usually solitary (in most species of shrubs), though there may also be two, e.g. in the lilac and bladdernut. Lateral buds are formed in the axils of the leaves and are alternately arranged, e.g. in the rose, currant, willow, or opposite, i.e. paired on either side of the twig, as in the common elder, cornelian cherry,

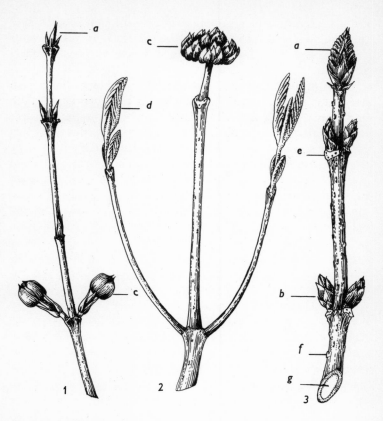

Fig. 8. Buds of woody plants: 1) cornelian cherry, 2) wayfaring tree, 3) common elder;
a — terminal bud, b — lateral bud, c — flower bud, d — naked bud, e — leaf scar, f — lenticels, g — pith.

privet, etc. In some species these buds are not always exactly opposite each other and are called subopposite, e.g. the spindle tree, privet and buckthorn. Flower buds vary greatly in shape, especially in the case of early flowering species such as cornelian cherry, Japanese quince, blackthorn and sea buckthorn.

In most woody plants the buds are clearly visible. Only in rare instances are they enclosed by the leaf stalk base and concealed from view until the leaf falls. Such buds are found, for instance, in the mock orange (*Philadelphus*).

Small, hard or leathery leaves known as scales protect buds against damage from heat, cold and drying winds. Only in rare instances are buds without scales and covered only with a thick pubescence, e.g. those of the wayfaring tree and alder buckthorn. These are called naked buds. Buds with scales covering only the bottom part and with the leaf tips showing are called semi-naked, e. g. those of the common elder and cotoneaster.

Discernible below the buds is the leaf scar where the leaf was attached to the twig. Leaf scars vary in size and often have a characteristic shape. The leaf scars of the common elder, red elder, staghorn sumach and bladdernut are quite large. Sometimes the part of the twig below the bud is swollen and this spot is called the peg.

In some woody plants a further good means of identification is the twig, the various distinguishing features being its thickness, colour, pubescence, thorniness, angularity and sometimes also the number of corky pores or lenticels.

Thorny or spiny twigs are characteristic of the barberry, gooseberry, blackberry, blackthorn, hawthorn, sea buckthorn, common buckthorn, box thorn, and all roses.

Slightly angular are the twigs of the common elder, red elder and water elder, markedly angular are those of the traveller's joy and common broom.

SHRUBS AND THEIR NATURAL ENVIRONMENT

The branch of science concerned with the interrelationships of living organisms and their environment is called ecology. The chief ecological factors that in great part determine the general distribution of the various tree and shrub species are temperature and moisture. Particularly great are the differences in the temperature requirements of the various species; that is the principal factor limiting their occurrence and determining the types that can be cultivated in a given environment.

The area where shrubs grow naturally in the wild is called the area of natural distribution and may best be depicted on a map. When we compare the areas of distribution of the various species it is evident that some require specific temperature levels since they occur, for instance, only in southern Europe or only in coastal regions or only in a continental climate. On the other hand, some are very adaptable as to climate and grow throughout most of Europe from southern Italy to the far north, often beyond the Arctic Circle. Examples include the dog rose, blackthorn, water elder and alder buckthorn.

Other shrubs extend far to the north but do not occur in southern Europe with its warm climate. Such typical northern species are the European black currant and willow spiraea. Still other species, e.g. the rhododendrons, green alder and rock currant, grow in the high mountain climate of central and western Europe but never occur in the north polar regions.

Some shrubs grow mainly in the part of western Europe with a constant mild oceanic climate but are absent in the continental areas with severe winter frosts. These include the English holly, hawthorn and common broom. Others are common shrubs of southern Europe but in central Europe are to be found only in warm, sheltered situations. In such localities they are often relics from the warmer period following the Ice Age when their area of natural distribution extended farther north, with only those growing in warmer situations surviving when the climate changed again. Examples are the cornelian cherry, barberry, bladder senna, box and traveller's joy.

Similarly, various shrubs also have differing requirements as to light. In general it may be said that in youth all woody plants, including shrubs, stand up better to shade than in old age. The onset of the fruit-bearing period and increasing age are accompanied by the need of more light. A second general rule is that the better the other conditions of a given site the less will be the plant's need of light. That means that in poorer climates or where soil is less fertile the need of light is greater providing there is adequate moisture. This is illustrated by the fact that woody plants tolerating moderate shade under optimal ecological conditions become light-loving plants in the northern areas of their distribution.

Light-loving shrubs that do not tolerate much shade are the barberry, dog rose, quince, common broom, smoke tree and tamarisk. On the other hand, there are shrubs that grow better in the shade of trees, e. g. the box, rhododendron, red dogwood and white dogwood, Oregon grape, common elder, privet, alder buckthorn and mezereon. The evergreen shrubs of this group should never be exposed to full sunlight because they are easily damaged during the sunny frosty days at the close of winter. On such days the temperature drops to minus 15°C at night and on a clear sunny day it may rise above 10°C on that side of the shrub that is turned towards the south and the leaves then begin to transpire. However, they are unable to obtain water from the frozen soil to replace that which has evaporated and the result is that later in spring they turn brown and dry up. For that reason shade-loving evergreen shrubs should never be planted in places fully exposed to sunlight from the south. Besides these groups there is still another that tolerates either shading from the side or moderate shade from above. It includes the hazel, green alder, traveller's joy, spindle tree, wayfaring tree, water elder and bladdernut.

It is also important to know which shrubs do well in dry locations and which require greater moisture. The first group includes the barberry, common cotoneaster, golden rain, bladder senna, box thorn and Japan rose, the second willows of shrub height, the alder buckthorn, red dogwood, water elder, French tamarisk and other shrubs. As regards underground water an important factor is whether it is running or stagnant water. Running underground water that is close to the surface has a beneficial effect on most trees and shrubs whereas stagnant underground water is tolerated only by shrubs that grow in swamps, e.g. the eared willow and alder buckthorn.

Also the fertility of the soil and its composition is an important factor influencing the occurrence and distribution of shrubs growing in the wild as well as the placing of shrubs under cultivation. Shrubs often found growing on sandy, light and less fertile soils include the barberry, common broom, bladder senna, pea tree, French tamarisk and service-berry. Heavy and more fertile soils are preferred by the honeysuckle, wayfaring tree, guelder rose, common elder, hawthorn, Oregon grape, medlar and other shrubs. Woody plants growing on poor, light soils include most members of the family *Leguminosae*. Their modest requirements and hardiness are made possible by their symbiotic association with the bacteria living in their root nodules. These are nitrogen-fixing bacteria, which increase the nitrogen content of the soil surrounding the roots and improve the nourishment of the shrub. Species that thrive in lime-rich soil include the barberry, cornelian cherry, common cotoneaster, red dogwood, hawthorn and privet; those that prefer acid soils include the common broom and rhododendrons.

In the wild these factors do not affect the plant singly but in combination, their influence thus being either neutralized or strengthened. For example, the composition of the soil and the humus content influence its moisture. For the planting of shrubs in parks and gardens the moisture and composition of the soil are not so important, as they can be easily adapted or changed. On the other hand, town plantings are being increasingly affected by new dangers such as air pollution, and these must be taken into account when selecting shrubs for the city park or garden.

GROWING AND PROPAGATION OF SHRUBS

As already stated, the seeds and fruits of shrubs are generally dispersed by animals, mainly birds. Less commonly are they spread by the wind, as is the case with seeds of the willow, green alder, lilac and mock orange. Most shrubs have fleshy fruits that the birds feed on, dispersing them either by dropping or wiping them from their beaks or in their excrement.

Shrubs multiply naturally by means of seeds and may also be propagated vegetatively i.e. by suckers, cuttings, grafting or budding. Various methods are suitable for the various species of shrubs, each method having advantages and disadvantages. Tender young seedlings require great care during the first two years, and plants from such seedlings may also grow slowly during this initial period, so it is some time before they can be transplanted to their permanent site. However, seedlings usually have good root anchorage and attain a greater age than alternatively propagated plants. Garden hybrids and forms with differently coloured flowers or foliage, larger fruit and different habit of growth cannot be relied upon to come true to type when raised from seeds. The surest way of propagating such forms is by vegetative means, either by division of roots, cuttings, layering, grafting or budding. This assures that the propagated variety will be the desired one.

Shrubs may be propagated by vegetative means with varying degrees of ease. In some species all one need do is cut off a branch, insert it in the ground and within one to two years it will grow into a young shrub that can be transplanted. Other species are better multiplied by summer cuttings of soft leafy shoots. Some shrubs cannot be multiplied by stem cuttings at all. In such cases it is necessary to use root cuttings or else propagate the shrubs by grafting or budding onto a suitable stock.

Raising from Seeds

The important thing is to gather the seeds at the right time, i.e. when they are ripe but not so ripe as to fall to the ground before harvesting. As a rule this period is not unduly short for the seed is mature one to three weeks before the fruit splits and can be gathered at any time during that interval. The only exceptions are certain shrubs where the seeds fall as soon as they are ripe and have a short period of germination, or else are eaten by animals (willows, hazel). In such cases it is necessary to keep an eye on the plant and gather the seeds as soon as they are ripe. In the case of shrubs with fruits that split open, the pods, capsules or follicles are gathered as soon as they begin to turn brown, before the seed is fully ripe. These are then placed in a dry airy place and left there until the seeds fall out. The seeds must then be cleaned and sorted, after which the best ones are either sown in the autumn or stored until spring. The best method of storage is in a sealed packet or glass container in a cool place with temperature slightly above zero ($2° — 5°C$). The seeds of fleshy fruits, berries, drupes and pomes present a greater problem. In this case it is best to place the fruits in warm water, crush them and pour the water off together with soft parts of the fruits floating on the surface. The seeds and parts of the fruits remaining are then spread out to dry on a sheet of paper. After they have dried, the seeds are easily separated and sown. Larger fruits such as common quince, Japanese quince and medlar are best cut open and the seeds removed by hand.

It is of great importance to know the right time for sowing. Small seeds, e.g. of rhododendron, deutzia and mock orange, are sown in spring (March—April). The seeds of shrubs that ripen in summer (currants, service-berry, honeysuckles, pea tree, etc.) should be sown immediately for they need a cool to cold period (winter) to break their dormancy and assure germination in spring. The seeds of certain *Leguminosae* with their harder seed coat should be briefly immersed in hot water (about 70°C) before sowing, for then they germinate sooner and more uniformly.

The larger seeds of such shrubs as hazel, cornelian cherry, dogwood, wayfaring tree, medlar, blackthorn, bladdernut, spindle tree, etc., which take longer to germinate, should be sown directly in the autumn or else stratified for the winter and sown the following spring. The advantage of stratifying is that birds and rodents do not have access to the seed bed or frame during the winter. Also a good protective measure against birds and the like is to sprinkle the dampened seeds with red lead before sowing.

Seeds are stratified by placing with a mixture of two parts sand and one part peat in alternating layers in pots, which are then stored in the cellar or some other cool room, with occasional watering to keep the substratum slightly damp. Seeds stratified in earth, peat or sawdust are more likely to rot if overwatered.

As winter draws to an end it is necessary to check the seeds often to see if they are germinating, in which case they must be pricked out into a frame or in pots.

Some seeds, even though stratified, will not germinate until the spring of the second year, e.g. the cornelian cherry, sometimes also the bladdernut, dogwood, wayfaring tree, English holly, staghorn sumach, etc. Such seeds should be stratified another year and in spring the pots in which they are stored should be put out in a shady spot and sunk in peat halfway to their rims, the peat being watered regularly to keep the substratum and seeds from drying out.

In spring the seeds are sown either into a frame or in pots filled with a mixture of equal parts loam, peat and sand. The seeds should be covered with a layer of soil one to two times their own thickness. For instance rhododendron seeds should be covered with a layer about 1 mm thick, those of the golden rain with a 5 mm layer, the bladdernut with a 10 mm layer, etc. The best temperature for seed germination is 16°C — 20°C. The seeds must be kept moist at all times, preferably with a fine rose can so that they are not washed out. Overwatering promotes the growth of mosses and lichens and can stifle the seedlings or even inhibit germination. It is a good thing to cover the pots containing the seeds with glass, turning it once each day to dry the condensation, and to protect them also from direct sunlight. During the first few months ater germination the seedlings should be lightly shaded against strong sunshine. The spring of the second year the seedlings are transplanted to a bed where they are left undisturbed for at least two years. At the end of that period, if strong enough, they are transferred to their permanent site. If the seedlings are too densely planted in the pot they should be pricked out some 2—3 centimetres apart as soon as the primary leaves appear and the root has not yet branched, being left thus until the following spring, when they are then transferred to the bed.

Propagation by Vegetative Means

Vegetative reproduction is a method commonly used in the propagation of shrubs because most species produce prolific shoots or root suckers. As a rule this method yields plants for setting out in permanent quarters in a shorter time and also makes it possible to propagate shrubs that do not set seeds. It is the only method that ensures that the new plants shall be true to type. Vegetative reproduction includes propagation by division, layering, cuttings, grafting and budding.

Propagation by Division of Roots and Layering

The simplest and easiest method of propagating shrubs is by division. This way, of course, it is possible to produce only one or at most several new individuals, but one great advantage is that they are usually sturdy enough to be planted out in the open immediately. This method can be used to propagate shrubs that continually shoot out new suckers from the base and have a tufted habit of growth. These include the Japanese quince, mock orange, Oregon grape, heath, snowberry, some species of spiraea, staghorn sumach, dogwood, Japan rose, raspberry, etc. The best time for division of roots is in the spring. The entire shrub is lifted from the soil and divided into several sections with a knife or a sharp spade or else some of the earth is worked away from the side of the shrub and the individual root suckers are separated from the mother plant. If the offshoot has an insufficiently developed root system it is advisable to plant it in a nursery bed and cut the top back hard to allow it to recover and grow.

Another easy method of propagation is layering, though this, too, produces only a limited number of new individuals. This method is based on the fact that if the young shoot or shrub is bent and inserted in the soil it will put forth roots. Some shrubs multiply in this manner in the wild, e.g. the blackberry, dogwood, etc. In gardening layering is used mainly for those shrubs that are not easy to propagate by cuttings or grafting. Layering may be carried out either on the spot where the shrub is growing or else in a special bed to which the shrub to be increased is transferred. One advantage of the latter is that it is possible to prepare a soil mixture suitable for propagation, i.e. a lighter, sandy soil, and that the shrubs can be spaced far enough apart. Young one-year shoots root best. For that reason, if the shrub does not have a sufficient number of long, one-year shoots close to the base it must first be cut back so that it produces new young shoots. The following spring these shoots are then bent, a portion is buried in the soil, but not too deeply, and the tip is brought up above the surface of the soil and tied to a peg so that it will grow upward. To keep the shoot securely in place it is fastened down with a wooden peg at the point of the bend which is then covered with a layer of soil, peat and sand to prevent drying. To promote the growth of roots a tongue-like incision is made in the wood at the point of contact with the ground or a narrow strip of bark is removed. It is beneficial to expose the layered branch to the sun because warmer soil promotes rooting. As a rule the branch puts out a good root system during the growing period so that it can be separated from the parent plant in November or early spring and transplanted to the bed. This method can be used for the propagation of various species of *Viburnum*, *Cydonia*, *Exochorda*, *Magnolia*, *Rhododendron*, and other shrubs not easy to propagate by cuttings.

A similar method, known as stooling, is used to increase choice varieties of the hazel or to produce a greater quantity of rootstocks for budding or grafting fruit trees. Shrubs to be increased are cut back close to the ground in early spring so that they will put out as many shoots as possible. As these shoots grow they are covered with a mound of soil up to about 30 centimetres high. During the summer the shoots put forth new roots and in the autumn the soil is removed and the rooted shoots are cut away from the parent shrub and planted out. This method is sometimes used to propagate certain varieties and species of *Philadelphus*, *Deutzia*, *Hydrangea* and *Syringa*.

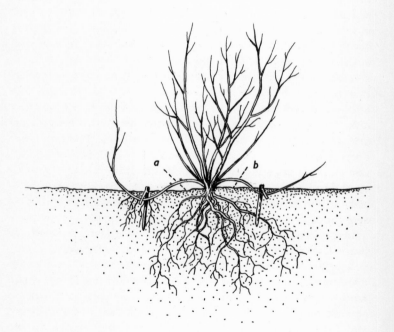

Fig. 9. Propagation of shrubs by layering: a,b — point where rooted shoots are cut off.

Propagation by Cuttings

This is the most commonly used method of propagating shrubs. Cuttings may be taken at two times: in winter, when the wood is hard and ripe, and in summer, when the young stems are soft and green. Winter or hardwood cuttings are the simplest and require no special equipment. All that needs to be done is to plant them out in nursery beds or frames. Summer or softwood cuttings require constant humidity and are placed in a propagating frame or greenhouse or in boxes covered with glass. Shrubs propagated mainly by winter cuttings include those that take root easily in the open (*Salix, Spiraea, Deutzia, Philadelphus, Lonicera, Ligustrum, Rosa, Ribes,* etc.).

Winter cuttings are taken from one-year shoots in early winter before the first frosts. The cuttings are usually 20—30 cm in length, the bottom cut being made just below a bud and the upper cut just above a bud. The bottom cut is made just below the bud because that is the spot where the cuttings put forth new roots most readily. For the same reason it is sometimes recommended to take cuttings with a heel, i.e. with a sliver of the old wood where the shoot arises. This method is used mainly in the case of shrubs that do not root readily for it is possible to make only a limited number of such cuttings. When taking winter cuttings the soft tops of the shoots are removed. The cuttings are either inserted immediately in a nursery bed or are tied in bunches of 25—50 and stored in moist sand in a cool shed or put in sand or peat out in the garden. In very cold areas they should be covered with a layer of leaves as protection against damage by frost. In early spring, as soon as weather permits, the cuttings are inserted in a nursery bed in rows spaced 20 cm apart. The distance between the individual cuttings in a row should be 7—10 cm. The cuttings are inserted up to 2/3rds of their length, directly in the soil by hand using a spade or dibber to make a hole. It is important that the lower end of the cutting be firmly surrounded by soil. In the case of thorny branches it is necessary first to remove the thorns that would hamper insertion. In the case of shrubs that do not root easily the lower tip of the cutting can be dipped in a hormone rooting preparation. Stimulators and instructions for their use may be normally purchased in any shop selling gardening supplies. Hardwood cuttings require little care. All that needs to be done is removal of weeds and watering during dry spells. Within three to four weeks a callus (healing tissue) forms on the bottom of the cutting and usually soon after the first roots appear. The roots of most hardwood cuttings are well established by early winter.

Summer or softwood cuttings are an even more effective means of propagation, used with shrubs that do not multiply well from winter cuttings, e.g. *Cytisus, Viburnum, Spiraea, Staphylea, Rhamnus*. Summer cuttings must be inserted in a greenhouse, frame, or box covered with glass because they wilt easily and require a moister atmosphere. Summer cuttings are taken from June to the end of August according to the nature and maturity of the shoots. Cuttings from evergreens are usually taken as late as August.

Summer cuttings are taken from spring shoots when they begin to turn woody at the base. They are shorter than winter cuttings, from 4 to 10 cm in length. The bottom cut is again made just below the bud, where new tissue is produced more readily. All leaves are removed from the bottom part of the cutting that is to be inserted into the rooting medium. If the remaining leaves are more than 8—10 cm long, it is best to shorten them by at least half to limit transpiration. The best rooting medium for cuttings is a mixture of one part gritty river sand and one part peat, on top of which is added a 1—1.5 cm layer of river sand. This is then well watered and lightly tamped down. The cuttings should be inserted to about 1/3rd of their length in holes made with a dibber slightly thicker than the cuttings and lightly firmed in. The bed or pot should then be well watered and covered with glass. Subsequently, the cuttings should be sprayed lightly from one to several times a day and shaded from full sun. After the callus or first roots appear watering should be gradually increased. Once the cuttings have rooted they should be hardened off in the autumn by removing the glass and left in the frame for the winter.

Propagation by Root Cuttings

Woody plants that throw out shoots from the roots may be propagated by root cuttings. This is a fairly simple method, which may be carried out during the dormant period when the gardener has the most time. Such plants as *Hippophae rhamnoides*, *Chaenomeles lagenaria*, *Rhus typhina*, *Rubus sp.* or *Campsis radicans* can be propagated in this way. It is best to take the cuttings in December before the soil freezes. The earth is removed from one side of the shrub to expose the roots and a certain number of these are cut off, but only so many as not to cause serious damage to the parent plant. Best of all are roots as thick as a pencil. These are then washed and cut with a sharp knife into sections of 6—8 cm in length, which are then planted in boxes or pots containing equal parts sand and peat. The root cuttings are inserted at an angle and care must be taken that this is done with the top part (the cut closer to the stem) up. The cuttings are then covered with a 1 cm layer of the same mixture. Afterwards, the soil is well watered and the box placed in a dark place with a temperature of about 15°C. The first buds appear in about four to five weeks, at which time the boxes are exposed to the light so that the shoots will be short and sturdy. The ensuing care is the same as with plants from stem cuttings.

Grafting and Budding

Another method of increasing certain shrubs and their garden varieties is grafting and budding, where part of the plant to be propagated, either a graft or a bud, is transferred and attached to well-rooted stock of a common species. For some shrubs and fruits this is practically the only and most reliable means of propagation (tea roses, lilac, magnolia, apples and pears).

The successful outcome of grafting and budding depends on the extent to which the severed tissues of the scion join with those of the stock to form a new individual. It is not only important that the scion be placed on the stock cambium to

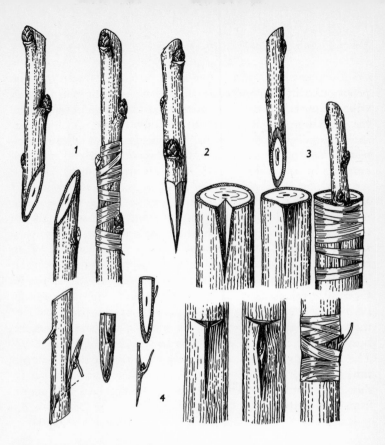

Fig. 10. Methods of grafting: 1) whip-grafting, 2) slit or notch grafting, 3) rind-grafting, 4) budding.

cambium and wood to wood, but also that their tissues have a mutual affinity. For this reason the scion and stock must be from allied species, preferably of the same genus or family. The best and most reliable stocks for various species according to expert literature and verified in practice are the hawthorn, quince, cherry plum, privet, wayfaring tree.

It is necessary to stress that care and precision are important requirements of grafting and budding. The knife used to prepare the scion and the stock must be well sharpened, the cuts must be straight and smooth and their surface must not be soiled by the fingers or otherwise.

The best time for grafting in the open is early spring (March to April), when the stocks begin to bud. In the greenhouse, where the scions are grafted onto potted and budding stocks, the best time is January and February. The branches for grafting are preferably cut about one month or more before grafting and heeled in against a shady wall or in the refrigerator. The actual scions are prepared from these branches just before grafting.

Several different forms of grafting are used in the propagation of shrubs. The simplest is whip or tongue grafting, employed where the stock and scion are of similar thickness. With this method the scion, cut downward at an angle, is placed against the stock, cut at a corresponding angle to the scion.

Slit or notch grafting is used when the diameter of the stock is several times greater than that of the graft. With this method a wedge-shaped incision is made in the stock and the scion, cut at an angle corresponding with that of the wedge-shaped incision, is fitted into the stock. It is also possible to merely make a straight cut in the stock and spread the tips apart to receive the scion.

Rind grafting is a method that can be employed only when the sap is already running in the stock and the bark can be loosened easily. With this method a T-shaped slit is made in the bark and the scion, cut with a thin tail, is slipped between the wood and the bark.

More detailed instructions concerning the various methods of grafting are to be found in every gardener's manual.

Another method of vegetative propagation is budding, a form of grafting used for roses, lilacs, medlars, hawthorns and other woody plants. The best time for this is summer (from late June till mid-September). A well-developed bud with a piece of leaf stalk and shield of bark is cut from the plant to be propagated. A T-shaped incision is made in the bark of the stock and the bud is then slipped between the bark and the wood. The bud should form a union with the stock within two to three weeks, manifested by the shedding of the small piece of leaf stalk. The bud usually remains dormant throughout the autumn and winter and does not start growing until the following spring. However, a percentage of early budded roses begin growing as soon as the bud is united.

Pruning and Rejuvenation

The finest and most abundant display of flowers are borne by shrubs that have ample young wood. Shrubs left untended rejuvenate themselves by throwing out new shoots from the base and it is therefore necessary to aid them in this process. Pruning should not be left until too late so as to prevent the need of removing wood that is very old, for the shortening of strong thick branches mars the shrub's overall appearance. A further rule of pruning is that one should maintain the natural habit and shape of the shrub as much as possible. Only in the case of neglected shrubs or ones with asymmetric growth are the branches cut back hard, i.e. all the branches are cut back to 10 cm above the ground. As a rule it then takes two to three years for the shrubs to attain a reasonable size to bear flowers. With tended shrubs old branches are removed regularly every two to three years. The time for pruning is the winter, but not when the temperature is below freezing point. Shrubs that put out leaves early in spring should be pruned earlier; those that put out leaves later may be pruned later — any time up to the beginning of May. Wherever possible, the cut is made just above the bud so that there will be no remains of the old, dead and dry wood above the new shoots.

Most shrubs need moderate pruning to encourage more vigorous growth and increase of flowers. Early flowering shrubs such as *Chaenomeles, Forsythia, Spiraea thunbergii, S. crenata, Prunus* spec. and the like should be pruned after the flowering period. Moderate pruning after flowering is also required at several-year intervals by *Syringa, Mahonia, Viburnum lantana* and other shrubs.

Shrubs bearing terminal panicles or racemes on strong summer shoots require harder pruning at the beginning of spring, otherwise they produce weak shoots and scanty blossoms. In such instances the shoots should be shortened to as much as half their length. This group includes mostly shrubs that do not flower until June, e.g. *Cytisus*, *Spiraea salicifolia*, *Spiraea japonica*, *Buddleia*, *Colutea*, *Ligustrum*, *Rosa rugosa* and remonant roses, *Lycium*, *Hibiscus*.

Likewise, old hedges beginning to thin markedly at the base should be pruned hard or cut back by one half.

PLATES

The following plates are arranged according to the taxonomic system. The reader, not experienced in systematics, will easily find every described species in the alphabetic index at the end of the book.

Key to symbols used:

♀ — female flowers

♂ — male flowers

Purple Osier

Salicaceae

Salix purpurea L.

The purple osier is a narrowly branched upright shrub growing to a height of 2—5 m. The stems are slender and flexible, coloured greenish brown in a shady location and purplish red in a sunny aspect. The pith of older shoots is a bright yellow. The buds on the twigs are narrowly conical, appressed, usually alternate, with at least one pair of opposite buds on each twig. The male and female flowers are borne on separate individuals and appear in early spring before the leaves, usually at the end of March. The male flower has only one double stamen with red anthers. The capsules mature at the end of May, when they split to release a number of white cottony seeds. The shrub is propagated by cuttings.

It grows near streams and water courses in both lowland and mountain areas. It is especially plentiful alongside mountain streams and often forms vast thickets on sandy and gravel alluvial deposits. The northern limit of its distribution extends as far as central Sweden. Its flexible branches are used in basket-making and cultivated varieties are grown specially for this purpose. It is also planted for short periods to improve dry sandy locations.

Leaves: Alternate, sometimes opposite, lanceolate, broadest above the middle, 4—9 cm long, with serrate margins in the upper third, blue-green undersurface.

Flowers: Dioecious, male and female flowers in catkins 2—3 cm long.

Fruit: Capsules borne in 3 cm-long spikes.

1 — buds,
2 — ♂ flowers,
3 — ♀ flowers,
4 — leaves,
5 — fruits

Common Osier

Salix viminalis L.

The common osier is a shrub growing from 2—6 m in height with stout, flexible, greenish-yellow stems tipped with silky hairs. The alternate buds are elongate, flat and coloured greenish brown. As in all species of willow they are covered by a single, cap-like scale. The dioecious flowers appear before the leaves at the end of March. The male flowers have two stamens. The capsules split to release the seeds at the end of May. It sprouts prolifically when pollarded and is propagated by cuttings.

The range of distribution embraces most of Europe, extending northward as far as the Arctic Circle. It is most abundant in lowland and hilly country but is absent at higher, mountain elevations. It forms thick stands on the banks of streams and large rivers and grows on gravel, sand and loam as well as boggy alluvial deposits. It requires abundant light and does not grow in closed stands. The long flexible shoots are used in basket-making and cultivated forms are specially grown for this purpose.

Leaves: Alternate, narrowly lanceolate, 11—20 cm long and 1—2 cm wide with coarsely wavy, curled margin and silvery, silky-hairy underside.
Flowers: Dioecious, short (2 cm), plump, yellowish catkins.
Fruit: Capsules in upright catkins.

1 — buds,
2 — ♂ flowers,
3 — ♀ flowers,
4 — leaves,
5 — fruits

Eared Willow

Salix aurita L.

The eared willow grows to 1—2 m in height, and is a densely branched shrub of upright habit. First year twigs are covered with a fine grey pubescence, later becoming brownish and smooth. The closely alternate buds are barrel-shaped and covered by a single scale. It derives its name from the kidney-shaped stipules arranged in pairs at the base of the leaves. The dioecious flowers appear in the second half of April and the seeds are released from the capsules in June. This species multiplies well from the seed but is less easy to propagate by means of cuttings.

This shrub grows wild throughout most of Europe, extending across Russia to Siberia. It is a typical inhabitant of wet and boggy locations with acid soil. It is found not only in swampy alder groves at lowland elevations, but also in marshy meadows in the foothills and mountains, even at elevations above 1000 m. In woodlands it grows in ditches alongside forest paths, in locations with a high level of underground water and in peat bogs. It is of little importance economically or as an ornamental but can be employed to afforest boggy locations and the banks of water reservoirs. The flowers are visited by bees.

Leaves: Alternate, obovate, broadest above the middle, size 2—5 by 1—2 cm with two persistent, kidney-shaped stipules at the base next to the stalk; wrinkled, mat green above, grey-hairy below, with irregularly toothed margins.
Flowers: Half as large as those of the sallow.

1 — buds,
2 — ♀ flowers,
3 — ♂ flowers,
4 — leaves,
5 — fruits

European Green Alder

Alnus viridis [CHAIX] DC.

Betulaceae

The green alder is a shrub branching from the base and attaining a height of 1—3 m. The male catkins are already visible in autumn. The twigs are flattened, brownish-green with whitish warts. The buds, unlike those of other alders, are stalkless, pointed, and coloured greenish brown. The catkins appear together with the leaves in April to May. The cone-like fruit is only 1 cm long and is a paler colour and less woody than that of the common alder*. The small-winged fruits are yellow-brown and resemble those of the birch.

It is a high-mountain shrub growing mainly in the Alps and Carpathians, where it forms dense thickets above the tree line at elevations of 1300 to 2200 m; it does not occur in Britain. The Urals and western and central Siberia are the home of a closely related geographical variety. The green alder stands up to abundant shade better than dwarf pine and is found mostly on north-facing, damper slopes. It is of importance in soil retention and prevents the formation of snow and rock avalanches. Alongside streams and gullies it occasionally descends to lower levels, where it covers uncultivated areas. It suckers freely when cut and also puts out root suckers, by which it is easily propagated.

Leaves: Alternate, ovate, bluntly pointed, 3—5 cm long, green above and below, with doubly toothed margin and rounded base.
Flowers: Monoecious; male catkins pendulous, violet-yellow, female catkins upright, green.

1 — buds,
2 — ♂ and ♀ flowers,
3 — leaves and cones,
4 — ripe cones,
5 — achene

* See 'Trees' in the same series.

Hazel

Corylus avellana L.

Betulaceae

The hazel is a shrub with straight shoots 3—6 m high, the bark smooth and brownish. The alternate buds are round ovate and covered with several scales. The male catkins are visible already in autumn, growing in length and maturing in March when their yellow pollen falls on the female, bud-shaped flowers with several slender carmine-red stigmas. By autumn the female flowers develop into a woody oval nut 1—1.5 cm long, enclosed in a green leafy cup. The kernel is oily and very tasty. Propagate by nuts sown in autumn. If stored dry and sown in spring germination is delayed until the second spring.

Widespread throughout most of Europe, its range extends northward as far as the 63rd parallel. In central Europe it grows mostly on the edges of forests, in hedgerows and in open woods up to elevations of 300—600 m. On limestone rock it grows up to elevations of 1000 m. It requires partial sunlight but will grow in drier situations and poorer soil. It yields flexible wood and charcoal.

Leaves: Alternate, obovate, 7—12 cm long, with heart-shaped notch at the base and shortly pointed apex; margin doubly toothed, veins prominent on the underside, glandular hairy, stalk 1—2 cm long and covered with hairs.

1 — buds,
2 — ♂ and ♀ flowers,
3 — leaves and fruits,
4 — nut with kernel

Common Barberry

Berberis vulgaris L.

The common barberry is a thorny bush, 1—2 m high, with upright branches slightly bent at the tip. The ovate buds, located in the axils of 1—7 branched thorns, are arranged in spirals on the yellow-grey shoots. The round, yellow flowers, composed of six sepals and six petals, appear at the end of May. The fruits are bright red, oblong berries, measuring 8—13 mm and borne in drooping clusters. Inside are 1—3 pip-like seeds. The berries ripen in September and often remain on the shrub until late in winter.

This is a warmth-loving shrub widespread in central and southern Europe. It grows in greatest abundance on rocky, especially limestone hillsides, at the margins of forests, in hedgerows and in pastures. A light-loving species, it stands up well to dry weather. Because it is a host plant of grain rust *(Puccinia graminis)* it is not welcomed in hedgerows and in the vicinity of fields and is therefore eradicated there. The wood of barberry is lemon yellow.

Popularly planted in parks and gardens as attractive thorny hedges are several colour varieties of the common barberry or the related species *Berberis thunbergii* with smaller, entire leaves.

Leaves: Alternate, longish ovate, 3—5 cm in length, borne in clusters, blade rounded at the apex, narrowly wedge-shaped at the base, margin sharply toothed with prominent veins on the underside.
Flowers: Yellow, in drooping clusters.
Fruit: Ovoid, red berries.

1 — buds,
2 — flowers,
3 — leaves and fruits,
4 — seed

Traveller's Joy

Clematis vitalba L.

Ranunculaceae

Traveller's joy is a climbing shrub attaching itself to the stems and branches of other woody plants with its leaf stalks and growing to a height of 6—8 m. The stem is angular in cross-section and covered with bark that peels off in long strips and may be as much as 2—3 cm thick. The whitish flowers, measuring 2 cm across, bloom in June and July; the achenes ripen in September and October and form heads with whitish feathery plumes. They remain on the bush until late in winter.

This shrub is a native of southern Europe and Asia Minor, growing in warm locations as far north as central Europe and England. It is found in greatest abundance on fresh, fertile soils in riverine woods, on the margins of forests and in shrub thickets. In the neighbourhood of villages it grows on walls and fences. As it does not tolerate full sun, it is desirable to shade at least the lower part of the shrub. Dry situations are likewise not suitable. In ornamental gardening it is used as rootstock for choice varieties and hybrids with large decorative blooms. In riverine woods it is sometimes a harmful plant because it bends and stifles young growing trees.

Leaves: Opposite, with 3—5 heart-shaped, long-stalked leaflets measuring 3—10 cm with coarsely toothed margins.
Flowers: With 4 whitish sepals, borne in sparse panicles.
Fruit: 4-mm achenes with feathery plumes.

1 — buds,
2 — leaves and flowers,
3 — ripening fruits,
4 — fruit,
5 — large-flowered hybrid

Virgin's Bower

Clematis viticella L.

Ranunculaceae

Virgin's bower is a climbing shrub growing to a height of only 3—4 m. The leaf stalks are twining and support the plant on fences and the stems of other woody plants. The bluish to reddish purple flowers appear in the axils of the leaves on stalks about 10 cm long from June to September. The sepals are petal-like. The seed-like achenes lack the feathery plumes characteristic of other clematis and ripen from August onwards.

A native of southern Europe and Asia Minor, this shrub grows on rocky hillsides and sun-warmed slopes. In central and western Europe it is often planted in parks and gardens. It is a light-loving plant but does not tolerate full sun and should therefore not be planted on house walls with a southern exposure. It is important to water the plant during dry spells. In the mid-19th century it was crossed with Asiatic *C. lanuginosa* and American species by the English gardener George Jackman, who bred a number of hybrids with large ornamental flowers.

Leaves: Opposite, simple to trifoliate, with entire or slightly lobed margin.
Flowers: Blue or red-purple, twice as large as those of traveller's joy.
Fruit: An achene measuring 8—10 mm with a bristle-like appendage.

1 — leaves and flowers,
2 — ripening fruits,
3 — ripe fruit head,
4 — fruit

Mistletoe

Viscum album L.

Mistletoe is an evergreen shrub with forked branches that is parasitic on trees. The stem is covered with yellow-green bark. The shrub grows to a height of about 50 cm and is almost circular in shape. It establishes itself on the branches of trees, which it penetrates with its roots, thereby obtaining the water and mineral substances it needs for growth. There are several varieties of mistletoe, distinguished according to the host plant on which they grow, e.g. fir, pine, and deciduous trees; these are always parasitic on the same species of tree and differ from each other morphologically, primarily by the width of the leaves.

Blooming early in spring from February to April, the flowers are borne in sessile clusters of 3—5. The fruits are berries which ripen in November to December and contain a sticky juice used at one time by fowlers to catch birds. It is a popular ornamental plant used to decorate homes during the Christmas season.

It grows in western, central and southern Europe and is mostly parasitic on fir and pine trees, and of the deciduous species on poplars, birches, maples, limes and fruit trees. Parasitic on oaks is the closely related yellow-berried mistletoe *(Loranthus europaeus)*, which is deciduous; this species does not occur in Britain, where mistletoe is occasionally found on oaks.

Leaves: Growing in pairs at the tip of forked twigs; evergreen, leathery, tongue-shaped, 4—6 cm long, with entire margin and parallel veins.
Flowers: Dioecious, small, yellow.
Fruit: A round, white berry measuring 6 mm.

1 — flowers,
2 — leaves and fruits,
3 — seed

Oregon Grape

Mahonia aquifolium NUTT.

The Oregon grape is a shrub of suckering habit, 1—1.5 m tall. It is a native of North America, where it grows in damp forests from California northward to British Columbia. The pinnate leaves, measuring about 20 cm, are a glossy dark green, turning shades of copper and bronze in winter. The yellow flowers, borne in clustered racemes, appear in April. The bluish berries containing 3—5 seeds ripen in August and are edible. They are also used in preserves and to colour wines.

This is a valuable, evergreen ornamental shrub, widely cultivated in the parks of western, central and eastern Europe. It is sufficiently resistant to frost even in northern Germany, being damaged by spring frosts only if planted in sunny situations. It grows best in partial shade and does well even in drier situations. It is readily propagated by means of seeds or more usually by root suckers. In the vicinity of housing developments and cemeteries it can be found growing semi-naturalized in hedgerows and woods. In parks it is planted as an evergreen ground cover and to form low evergreen hedges; it is also planted for game cover.

Leaves: Alternate, pinnate, composed of 5—9 sharply toothed leaflets, evergreen, semi-leathery and glossy.
Flowers: Yellow, borne in upright racemes.
Friut: Blue-black berries covered with a bloom.

1 — flowers,
2 — leaves and fruits,
3 — fruit and seed

Mountain Currant

Ribes alpinum L.

Grossulariaceae

The mountain currant is a thornless shrub of upright habit growing to a height of 1—2.5 m. The stems are yellow-brown with bark that tends to crack. The buds are longish ovate, pointed and coloured light brown. The flowers appear in May. They are generally dioecious, with the male and female flowers borne on separate plants. The clusters of male flowers are half as long as the female clusters. The red berries measure about 7 mm and are borne in clusters of 1—5 berries. They ripen in July and have an insipid taste.

It grows in central and southern Europe, extending northward as far as the Baltic Sea to Leningrad and southern Finland and Sweden. Requiring partial shade, it grows in damp, rocky situations in forests from hilly country to high mountain elevations above 1000 m, but will grow in poorer and drier soils. Because it stands up well to pruning it is used in gardens and parks to form low hedges and shrubbery borders. It is well propagated both by means of seeds and winter and summer cuttings.

Leaves: Alternate, 3—5 lobed, 3—5 cm large, the lobes pointed, margin toothed, stalk covered with glandular hairs.
Flowers: Greenish yellow, borne in upright, many-flowered racemes — male flowers 20—30 and female flowers 2—5 to a cluster.

1 — buds,
2 — flowers,
3 — leaves and fruits,
4 — fruit with seeds

Rock Currant

Ribes petraeum WOLF

Grossulariaceae

The rock currant is a thornless shrub of upright habit growing to a height of 1.5—2 m. The stems are reddish brown with bark that tends to peel; the buds are dark brown, ovate. The reddish flowers appear at the end of May, the red, slightly sour berries in drooping clusters ripen in August and the seeds are dispersed by birds.

This shrub grows in the high mountains of southern and central Europe. It is plentiful, for instance, in the Alps and the Carpathians, where it grows up to 1700 m above sea level in rocky, sufficiently damp situations. It is the parent of numerous cultivated varieties grown for their fruit in gardens and orchards. It is a close relative of *R. spicatum* (the red currant), which grows mainly in northern Europe and Siberia, and of *R. rubrum*, which is distributed throughout the mountain areas of France and Belgium. All three species are parents of the large-berried hybrids grown in European gardens for their fruit.

Leaves: Alternate, with 3—5 pointed lobes, 5—9 cm long, margin sharply toothed, underside pubescent.
Flowers: Hermaphrodite, bell-shaped, reddish, borne in drooping racemes.
Fruit: Red berries measuring 6 mm.

1 — buds,
2 — flowers,
3 — leaves and fruits

Black Currant

Ribes nigrum L.

The black currant is a 1—1.5 m high shrub of broadly branching habit. The twigs are comparatively stout, greyish, and give off an unpleasant scent when cut. The buds are ovate, pale grey, on short stalks. The hermaphrodite red-green flowers appear in May. The black berries ripen in August.

It grows mainly in northern Europe and Siberia, where it occurs in woods, extending northward even beyond the Arctic Circle. In central and western Europe it is occasionally found growing in damp situations in woods alongside rivers. It is widely cultivated in gardens and fruit orchards, and in some places is found growing wild from seeds dispersed by birds. The black currant is a frost-resistant shrub requiring partial shade and greater soil moisture. Its high content of Vitamin C is the reason why it is widely grown in gardens, the fruits being used to make wine and preserves.

It is not welcomed in woodlands because as an intermediary host it promotes the spread of fungus disease by *Peridermium strobi* to the Weymouth pine and for this reason related species of currant are being systematically exterminated in the forests of Canada and the United States.

Leaves: Alternate, 5-lobed (3-lobed), 5—10 cm long, margin toothed, underside spotted with yellow glands.
Flowers: Reddish or brownish green, borne in 5—10 flowered, drooping racemes.
Fruit: Black, 1 cm-large berries.

1 — buds,
2 — flowers,
3 — leaves and fruits,
4 — seed

Gooseberry

Grossulariaceae

Ribes grossularia L.
(*Syn. Ribes uva-crispa* [L.] SM.,
Grossularia reclinata MILL.)

The gooseberry is a thorny, 0.7—1.2 m high shrub of broadly spreading habit with pendent shoots. The twigs are pale grey. The ovate buds are subtended by single or 3-branched thorns placed at right angles to the twig. The leaves appear early in spring (in March) and the hermaphrodite flowers in April. The sweet fleshy fruit with a greenish to reddish tinge ripens in July. The plant can be propagated by means of seeds and also by means of hardwood winter cuttings.

Widespread throughout most of Europe from the Pyrenees to the Caucasus, it extends northward to latitude 63° North in southern Scandinavia. In central Europe it grows in lowland and hilly country at the margins of forests or in broadleaved woods. In the mountains it is found at elevations as high as 800—1000 m. It is especially plentiful on rocky slopes. It is widely cultivated for its sweet fruit and many large-berried varieties have been bred.

Leaves: Alternate, 3—5 lobed, 2—5 cm long, with heart-shaped base. The lobes coarsely toothed, more bluntly tipped than in *R. alpinum.*
Flowers: Green to pinkish, borne in clusters of 1—3 flowers.
Fruit: Round to barrel-shaped berries, 1 cm large.

1 — buds,
2 — flowers,
3 — leaves and fruits,
4 — fruits of cultivated varieties

Deutzia

Saxifragaceae

Deutzia scabra THUNB.

Deutzia is a shrub of upright habit with numerous branches 1.5—2.5 m high. Young shoots are covered with star-shaped hairs, older branches with brownish bark that peels off in bands. The buds are small, ovate, pointed. The whitish flowers are borne in 6—12 cm long clusters on the tips of lateral twigs and bloom in June. The roundish, 6 mm capsules ripen and split in October.

A native of China and Japan, it is today widely cultivated in the parks of western and central Europe. It derives its name from Johann van der Deutz (1743—88), a Dutch patron of botany. It is an ornamental shrub highly prized for the colour and abundance of its flowers. In parks it is planted either as a solitary specimen or in taller hedges and shrubbery. It tolerates moderate shade and does not require much soil moisture. In locations subject to frost and in severe winters it tends to be partially damaged by frost. Propagation from seed is quite laborious and therefore it is usually increased either by means of softwood cuttings in summer or hardwood cuttings in autumn. The pink or double-flowered forms are especially prized in parks.

Leaves: Opposite, longish ovate, 3—9 cm in length, with pointed tip, finely toothed margin, scabrous above and pubescent on the upright racemes.
Flowers: White to pinkish flowers with ragged petals borne in upright racemes.

1 — buds,
2 — flowers and leaves,
3 — double-flowered form,
4 — fruits

Mock Orange

Philadelphus coronarius L.

The mock orange attains a height of 2—3 m and is of upright habit. The buds are opposite and small, in summer concealed beneath the broad leaf base; the twigs are dark brown. The flowers, which appear in June, are white and have a sweet scent resembling that of the orange blossom, hence its name. The capsules containing a large number of tiny seeds ripen in October.

This shrub is a native of southern Europe but has been cultivated in western Europe since the 16th century. It was once a very popular shrub for parks and gardens in western and central Europe and is completely resistant to frost. It is moderate in its requirements of soil richness and moisture and also tolerates shade, though it then bears fewer blossoms. It is planted either as a solitary specimen, to form thick hedges or in shrub borders, where, being spaced farther apart, the individual shrubs retain their characteristic habit of growth and bear a greater profusion of flowers. Nowadays many Asiatic species and hybrids have superseded *P. coronarius* in gardens.

Leaves: Opposite, broadly ovate, measuring 4—8 cm, the upper part of the blade with sharply toothed margin, the lower part with entire margin.
Flowers: White, fragrant, measuring 2—3 cm, borne in 5—7 flowered racemes.
Fruit: 8 mm long, four-valved capsules.

1 — buds,
2 — leaves and flowers,
3 — fruits

Willow Spiraea

Spiraea salicifolia L.

Rosaceae

The willow spiraea is an erect suckering shrub growing to a height of 1—2 m. The twigs are yellow brown, the buds small (2—3 mm) and bluntly ovate. Old shoots are dark brown and tend to peel. The dense spiky panicles of tiny pink, sometimes white, flowers do not appear until June and July. The small seed pods mature from the end of July to September, when they split to release the minute seeds.

This is a northern shrub growing from eastern Europe across Siberia as far as Japan. In central and western Europe it is cultivated in parks and gardens and may be found naturalized in thickets alongside streams and at the edges of woods. It is a sun-loving shrub that is completely frost-resistant and requires ample soil moisture. It is readily propagated by means of summer and winter cuttings. Very similar in habit of growth and flowers are the North American species *S. tomentosa* and *S. douglasii*, which have leaves with grey-felted underside.

Leaves: Alternate, lanceolate, 4—8 cm long with sharply toothed margin and prominent veins on the underside.
Flowers: Pale pink, borne in dense terminal, cylindrical spikes 5—10 cm long.
Fruit: Numerous tiny brownish follicles.

1 — buds,
2 — leaves and flowers,
3 — fruits

Vanhoutt Spiraea

Spiraea x *vanhouttei*

Rosaceae

This spiraea is a hybrid shrub, a cross between two Asian species: *S. cantoniensis* x *S. trilobata*. Of arching habit, it attains a height of 1.5—2 m. The twigs are brownish, the buds small and pointed. It is covered with small flat clusters of white flowers in late May and the first half of June, the fruits maturing and splitting at the end of July.

This is a very decorative and profusely flowering shrub widely cultivated in the parks of western and central Europe. It is planted either as a solitary specimen or in groups in a shrub border. The wealth of flowers is influenced by the amount of light, otherwise the shrub does not require particularly rich or moist soil. It is easily propagated by means of softwood and hardwood cuttings.

Early spring (April) is the time when flowers are borne by the related species *S. thunbergii*, *S. arguta* and *S. crenata*.

Leaves: Alternate, ovate, 3—5 lobed, 3—4 cm long, with toothed margin and blue-green undersurface.
Flowers: White, about 8 mm, borne in rounded cymes.
Fruit: Tiny reddish brown follicles.

1 — buds,
2 — flowers and leaves,
3 — fruits

1

2

3

Raspberry

Rubus idaeus L.

The raspberry grows to 1—2 m in height with erect as well as arching shoots. The shoots are two-year growths bearing only leaves the first year, flowering and fruiting in the second and dying off by winter. Coloured brown, they are covered with soft spines. The whitish flowers appear in May and June. The fruits ripen in July and August, after which they fall to the ground. Unlike the blackberry, the fruit of the raspberry is easily separated from the receptacle. Ripe berries are eaten by birds and animals and the small seeds are dispersed far and wide in their droppings.

This woodland shrub is widespread in western, central and northern Europe. It grows both in lowlands and on mountains up to elevations of 1800 m. It requires abundant light and therefore is most plentiful in forest clearings and at the margins of woods where there is good soil rich in humus. It is easily and quickly propagated by root suckers. The berries are used to make juices, desserts and jams. Cultivated varieties with large berries are grown in gardens and as a field crop.

Leaves: Alternate, pinnate, composed of 3—5 ovate leaflets with toothed margins and white-felted undersurface.
Flowers: White, fairly small, borne in loose, pendent clusters.
Fruit: Compact, rounded clusters of small red drupes.

1 — buds,
2 — flowers and leaves,
3 — twig with fruits,
4 — fruit,
5 — receptacle

Blackberry or Bramble

Rosaceae

Rubus fruticosus L.

The blackberry is a shrub reaching 1—1.5 m with arching or trailing shoots coloured green to wine red and covered with straight or hooked spines. Most of the leaves remain green throughout the winter. The pink or white flowers appear in July to August and the fruits ripen in September–October. The colour of the fruit changes as it ripens from green to red and black. The berries of this species are firmly attached to the receptacle so that, unlike the raspberry, when ripe they are plucked off together.

This is a large species comprising several hundred subspecies distributed throughout Europe, Asia and America. It grows in western, central and northern Europe, its range extending eastward to the Volga River. It is plentiful in lowlands and hilly country but does not grow at elevations above 800 m. It is found on the edges of forests, by the wayside and also in open woods, for it requires less light than the raspberry. It is especially fond of heavier and moist soils. In woodlands it often forms impenetrable thickets. It is usually propagated by means of natural tip layering.

Leaves: Alternate, five-foliate, terminal leaves on flower shoots trifoliate. Leaflets ovate, with toothed margin, spiny stalk and spiny venation.
Flowers: White, 5-merous, 2 cm, borne in loose panicles.
Fruit: Compact rounded clusters of small black drupes.

1 — winter twig,
2 — flowers and leaves,
3 — fruits

Dog Rose

Rosaceae

Rosa canina L.

The dog rose is a shrub growing to 1.5—3 m in height with erect as well as arching branches. The buds are small and reddish, the twigs greenish, with hooked thorns which can be easily removed. The flowers appear at the end of May and in June. The fruits, which ripen in October, are fleshy and edible and contain a large number of angular seeds measuring about 3 mm. They are rich in Vitamin C and are used to make wine, and for rose hip syrup.

Widespread throughout most of Europe, it grows in central Europe from lowland to mountain elevations up to 1000 m. It occurs in abundance at the edges of woods, in thickets on sun-warmed hillsides, by the wayside and in pastures. It is most plentiful in warmth-loving communities on dry, sunny banks. It requires abundant light and loamy soils, but does not need much moisture. Propagation is by means of seeds and root suckers. It is a colonist on grazed hillsides, preparing the way for the growth of woodland trees, which are able to gain a foothold as its thorns keep grazing animals at bay. In gardening it is used as rootstock for cultivated varieties of hybrid tea and other roses.

Leaves: Alternate, pinnate, 7—12 cm, composed of 5—7 ovate leaflets with doubly toothed margin. Two firmly attached stipules at the base of the leaf, main stem spiny.
Flowers: Pink, measuring 4—5 cm.
Fruit: Red, ovate hip, 1.5—2 cm, with curving sepals at the tip.

1 — buds,
2 — leaves and flowers,
3 — fruits,
4 — fruit with seeds

Burnet Rose

Rosaceae

Rosa spinosissima L.
(Syn. *Rosa pimpinellifolia* L.)

The Burnet rose is an upright shrub reaching 0.7—2 m in height. The shoots are densely covered with thin, straight thorns and needle-like bristles. The fairly large flowers bloom in May and June. The rounded blackish hips, about 1 cm across, with erect, persistent sepals at the tips, ripen in September.

Its widespread distribution extends from central Europe across the Ukraine and Siberia to China. It grows mostly in warmth-loving plant communities on rocky (especially limestone) banks with sunny aspect, but also does well on coastal sand dunes. It is a widely variable species, the many varieties including ones with rich yellow or salmon pink flowers and also one with double blooms. Because of its ornamental leaves and small size it is often planted in parks and in hedges. Propagation is chiefly by means of cuttings and root suckers. Fairly plentiful in the mountains of central and southern Europe is the related species *R. pendulina* (alpine rose) with sparse covering of thorns on the bottom part of the stem, bright red flowers and round, light red hips.

Leaves: Alternate, pinnate, measuring 4—6 cm and composed of 5—11 round to ovate leaflets with toothed margins.
Flowers: Creamy white, rarely pink, 2—5 cm, solitary, on longish stalks.
Fruit: Round, blackish brown hips.

1 — winter twig,
2 — leaves and flowers,
3 — fruits

Romanus Rose

Rosaceae

Rosa rugosa THUNB.

The Romanus rose reaches 1—2 m in height and has numerous shoots densely covered with thorns of varying size. The buds are ovate and reddish. The flowers bloom from the middle of June to August. The large, broad hips are brick red, turning purplish red when ripe in October, with long, erect sepals at the tips.

A native of the Far East, it grows from Kamchatka to Japan, Korea and northern China. It is most plentiful in coastal areas in river valleys in sandy situations. Nowadays it is widely cultivated in western and central Europe for its large, decorative and fragrant flowers, and it is completely frost-resistant. This species also includes varieties with double red as well as white blooms, e.g. 'Rubro-plena', 'Alba' and 'Albo-plena'. This rose has been crossed with other roses to produce several ornamental hybrids and varieties. It produces a great many root suckers, thereby spreading to form large groups and thickets. In some parts of Europe it has become naturalized. The hips are rich in Vitamin C.

Leaves: Alternate, pinnate, measuring 10—20 cm and composed of 5—9 thick, wrinkled, ovate leaflets with toothed margins.
Flowers: Carmine red, 6—8 cm across.
Fruit: Round, red hips, 2.5 cm in diameter.

1 — winter twig,
2 — flower,
3 — leaves and fruits,
4 — fruit with seeds

92

Blackthorn

Prunus spinosa L.

Blackthorn is a densely branched thorny shrub growing to a height of 1—5 m. The bark on the stem is blackish-brown and the lateral twigs have a terminal spine. The buds are small and ovate; the flower buds are generally borne in dense clusters on short twigs. The whitish flowers appear in April—May before the leaves. The fruits, known as sloes, ripen in September—October and are astringent, becoming tastier after the first frosts. The brown, pitted seed is difficult to separate from the pulp.

This shrub is widespread throughout most of Europe, its range extending northward to the 68th parallel and south-east to Asia Minor. In central Europe it is most plentiful in warm, wine-growing areas, where it forms dense thickets on dry, sunny banks. It has a richly branching root system and puts out root suckers freely, for which reason it is used to strengthen rocky banks and in the afforestation of barren slopes in karst areas. It is a widespread hedgerow plant as well. It occurs at elevations up to 600—700 m. Its thick, spiny branches provide a good shelter for small birds. The fruit is used for medicinal purposes and to make wine and dyes.

Leaves: Alternate, longish elliptical, 2—5 cm long, with wedge-shaped base and toothed margin.
Flowers: White, 5-merous, 1—1.5 cm, mostly growing in clusters,
Fruit: 1 cm, blue-black berry covered with a waxy bloom.

1 — buds,
2 — flowers,
3 — leaves and fruits,
4 — fruit with seed

Medlar

Rosaceae

Mespilus germanica L.

The medlar is a broad-spreading shrub or small tree, 3—6 m in height. The stem may be as much as 20 cm in diameter. The shoots are felted grey-brown, older branches are grey and covered with short, solitary spines. The fruits are apple-shaped, 3 cm across, flattened at the top and terminated by long sepals. When ripe, they turn brown and contain 5 hard angular seeds.

It is a native of Asia Minor, Iran and Caucasia, where it grows on richer soils in open broadleaved woods. It tolerates moderate shade. Cultivated varieties of this species are widely planted in the parks and gardens of central and western Europe. Unlike the wild plant these do not have spines and their fruits are much larger, up to 5 or 6 cm across. Newly matured fruits have a bitter taste; they are eaten and processed after the advent of frosts when the pulp softens and turns brown. Propagation is by means of root suckers; cultivated varieties may be grafted onto hawthorn. The medlar interbreeds with hawthorn and several hybrids between the two are known.

Leaves: Alternate, longish elliptical, 7—12 cm long, upper third of blade with finely toothed margin, lower part of blade with entire margin, underside felted grey-green.
Flowers: White, solitary, 3 cm across.

1 — buds,
2 — flowers,
3 — leaves and fruit,
4 — seed

Quince

Cydonia oblonga MILL.
Syn. (*Cydonia vulgaris* PERS.)

The quince is a tree-like shrub growing to a height of 2—7 m. The shoots and buds are felted, older branches are glabrous. The whitish flowers have a felted calyx and appear in May after the leaves. The unripe fruits are also felted, becoming smooth and turning lemon yellow when they ripen in October; these have a pleasant scent and are terminated by large, pointed sepals. Cultivated varieties bear fruits from 5 to 11 cm across. These are either pear-shaped — *C. o. pyriformis* or apple-shaped — *C. o. maliformis* and contain a large number of brown seeds measuring 4—6 mm.

A native of the area bordering the Caspian Sea, it grows on sandy and loamy soils around lakes as well as on dry banks. In central and western Europe it is cultivated in parks and gardens for its fruits and as an ornamental species. It grows best in a sunny spot, and tolerates dry situations. In Europe it is frost-resistant only in warmer regions. The fruits are edible and used either raw or cooked. Propagation is by means of seeds or green cuttings.

Leaves: Alternate, ovate, 6—11 cm long, with short tips, entire margins and grey-felted undersurface.
Flowers: Solitary, 5-merous, white to pinkish, measuring 4—5 cm.
Fruit: Pear-shaped or apple-shaped, 2—4 cm large.

1 — buds,
2 — flowers,
3 — leaves and fruit,
4 — fruit with seeds

Japanese Quince or Japonica

Chaenomeles lagenaria KOIDZ.
(Syn. *Chaenomeles speciosa* NAKAI,
Chaenomeles japonica [THUNB.] LINDL.)

Rosaceae

The Japanese quince is a thorny shrub with several main stems reaching 1—2.5 m. One-year shoots are glossy greenish brown, older ones dark brown. The buds are squat and reddish, the flower buds twice as large as the leaf buds. The pink to dark red flowers, about 4 cm in diameter, appear from December to April, the earliest ones appearing before the leaves. The yellow ovoid fruits, without any sepals, ripen in autumn and remain on the shrub until winter. They are rich in Vitamin C, have a pleasant aromatic scent, and can be used in making preserves. The ovary contains a large number of brown, apple-pip-like seeds.

This shrub is a native of the Shantung Province in China but has been cultivated in Japan for centuries. It is widely grown in the parks and gardens of central and western Europe for its lovely flowers. It also stands up well to temperatures of minus 20°C and grows on drier soils; however, it requires a sunny aspect to produce a profusion of flowers. It is readily propagated by means of seeds and also throws up root suckers. Solitary specimens are very ornamental but it is equally well suited for the formation of thick thorny hedges.

Leaves: Alternate, elliptical, 3—8 cm long, pointed, glossy dark green above, glabrous below, with toothed margins and two stipules at the base.
Flowers: Scarlet, 5-merous, 2—4 cm across.
Fruit: Ovoid, quince-like, 4—5 cm in diameter.

1 — winter twig,
2 — flowers,
3 — fruit and leaves,
4 — fruit with seeds

Cotoneaster

Rosaceae

Cotoneaster integerrima MED.
(Syn. *Cotoneaster vulgaris* LINDL.)

Cotoneaster grows to 1 or 2 m in height and is a densely branched shrub with arching shoots. One-year twigs are thin, reddish-brown and felted near the tip. The buds are of irregular shape, with the tips of the felted leaflets projecting between the opened scales. The inconspicuous flowers appear in May after the leaves; the red fruits, containing 2—3 flat seeds, ripen in August.

This shrub grows in western, central and eastern Europe, its range extending northward to central Scandinavia. (Found in similar situations in southern Germany and the Carpathians is the closely related species *C. tomentosa*.) It occurs primarily on dry, rocky hillsides; on limestone substrates it may be found even at elevations above 1500 m. It is a light-demanding species and resistant to drought. It is best propagated by means of seeds. The lovely foliage, delicate flowers and red fruits are valued for ornamental plantings. Preferred for parks are the more ornamental species from China with their greater profusion of flowers and fruits *(C. bullata, C. franchetii, C. dielsiana, C. multiflora)*, which are often raised from cuttings.

Leaves: Alternate, ovate, 2—3 cm, pointed, with entire margin and grey-felted underside.
Flowers: Small, bell-shaped, white, tinted pink, borne in clusters of 2—5 on short stems.
Fruit: Red, round, 8 mm in diameter.

1 — buds,
2 — leaves,
3 — flowers,
4 — fruits,
5 — seed

Service-berry or Snowy Mespilus

Rosaceae

Amelanchier ovalis MED.
(Syn. *Amelanchier vulgaris* MOENCH.,
Amelanchier rotundifolia DUM.)

The service-berry is a slender shrub with upright branches reaching 1—3 m in height. The stem is covered with blackish bark, the shoots are slender and reddish brown, the buds are violet-red and narrowly conical, terminating in a point. Emerging shoots are white tomentose. The whitish flowers, 2.5 cm in diameter, appear at the beginning of May together with the leaves. The edible fruits with their juicy pulp ripen in August, and are eaten by birds. Inside are 5—10 flat, sickle-shaped seeds. The shrub often produces root suckers.

It is widespread in southern and central Europe, its range extending eastward to Asia Minor and the Caucasus. In central Europe it is found in the mountains in limestone areas between 900 and 1500 m, and occurs at lower elevations farther north, e.g. in the Rhineland, where it grows in oak stands. It is a light-loving species and stands up well to long dry spells. Widely cultivated in European parks are the North American species *A. laevis* and *A. canadensis*, which grow to heights of 6—10 m.

Leaves: Alternate, ovate, 2—4 cm, with rounded apex, serrate margin, white-felted underside becoming glabrous with age.
Flowers: White, with narrow petals, borne in meagre racemes.
Fruit: Blue-black, 8 mm long, with large sepals.

1 — buds,
2 — leaves and flowers,
3 — fruits,
4 — seeds

Midland Hawthorn

Crataegus laevigata L.

Rosaceae

The hawthorn is a shrub growing to a height of 3—10 m and sometimes attaining the dimensions of a tree. The bark is smooth and grey, older bark is cracked. One-year shoots are olive-brown, older twigs grey and spiny. The reddish, round buds are located in the axils of the spines. The whitish flowers, which have a strong smell, appear in May. The fruit ripens in September—October. It has a characteristic crater-like hollow at the top and contains two stones.

This shrub is fairly widespread in western and central Europe, where it grows in riverine woods, at the margins of forests, in pastures and on shrubby banks. In the mountains it is found at elevations above 1000 m. It prefers heavy, loamy soils with calcium carbonate and grows well even in partial shade. The related *C. monogyna* is a thorny shrub used for hedges and is a good shelter for songbirds. The pink, red and white double-flowered varieties are often planted in parks and avenues. The single-flowered kinds are easily propagated by means of seeds; the double ones must be grafted. This species has deeply lobed leaves and one-seeded fruit.

Leaves: Alternate, ovate, 2—5 cm, shallowly lobed into 3 parts, with toothed margin, dark green upper surface and wedge-shaped base; two deciduous, kidney-shaped stipules.
Flowers: White, 5-merous, borne in upright cymes.
Fruit: Red, barrel-shaped pome, 8 mm large.

1 — buds,
2 — flowers,
3 — leaves and fruits,
4 — seeds,
5 — the common hawthorn
(*Crataegus monogyna*)

1

2

3

4

5

Broom

Sarothamnus scoparius WIMM.
(Syn. *Cytisus scoparius* LINK.)

Broom is a twiggy shrub with erect branches growing to 1—3 m. The twigs are green, angular, sparsely covered with leaves. The buds are small, round and paired. Broom has a tap root penetrating to a great depth and numerous lateral roots with root nodules containing nitrogen-fixing bacteria.

The natural area of distribution embraces western and central Europe. It does not thrive in neutral and alkaline soils, exhibiting better growth on acid substrates. It is found mostly in sandy and rocky situations by the wayside, on nonfertile soils, at the edges of forests and in heaths. It requires sunlight but will grow on drier and poorer soils. It occurs from lowland to hilly country and may be damaged by severe frosts. It enriches the soil with nitrogen and in winter is a source of food for hares and deer. Profusely flowering yellow and red varieties are cultivated in gardens.

Leaves: Alternate, upper ones on the shoots simple, lower ones trifoliate, 1.5 cm large; margin entire, underside pubescent.
Flowers: Yellow, pea-like, 2 cm large, borne singly or in pairs in the axils of the leaves.
Fruit: A black, flat legume, 4—6 cm long.

1 — winter twig,
2 — flowers,
3 — leaves and fruits,
4 — legume,
5 — seed

Pea Tree

Leguminosae

Caragana arborescens LAM.

The pea tree is a 2—6 m high shrub of upright habit with several stems covered with smooth, grey-green bark. The twigs are also green. On either side of the buds are two spiny stipules. The yellowish flowers open at the end of May. The pods ripen at the end of July, when they split and twist along the axis, ejecting the seeds several feet away. The seeds are kidney-shaped, round in cross section, yellow-brown, 4 mm long. They can be sown immediately in July or the following spring; they retain their power of germination for many years.

This shrub is a native of Siberia and Mongolia but for several centuries past has been cultivated in the parks and gardens of central and western Europe, where individual specimens also revert to the wild state. In its native home it grows mostly on sandy alluvial deposit and rocky banks. In central Europe it is completely frost-resistant, stands up well to dry spells and thrives on poorer soils. It tolerates moderate shade. As an ornamental it is suitable for individual planting, in groups in shrub borders and for hedging. Often planted in parks is the weeping form, *C. a.* 'Pendula'. The pea tree is visited by bees. It is readily propagated by means of seeds.

Leaves: Alternate, even-pinnate, composed of 8—14 leaflets, 6—9 cm long. Leaflets elliptical, with entire margin, the principal vein terminating in a spine.
Flowers: Yellow, pea-like, 2 cm large, with longish stalks.
Fruit: Brown, 5 cm long, cylindrical pods.

1 — buds,
2 — flowers,
3 — leaves and fruits,
4 — legume with seed

Laburnum or Golden Rain

Leguminosae

Laburnum anagyroides MED.
(Syn. *Laburnum vulgare* GRIESEB.)

Laburnum is a 5—7 m shrub often grown as a tree in gardens. The bark is smooth and greenish brown, the shoots greyish green, covered with silvery hairs. The racemes of yellow flowers appear at the end of May in golden cascades giving the impression of 'rain', hence the shrub's name. The flat, silvery hairy pods are slightly sickle-shaped. They mature at the end of September and remain on the shrub until spring. The seeds are blackish brown, kidney-shaped, and measure 4 mm. All parts of the plant, from leaves to fruit, are poisonous (they contain the alkaloid cytisine) However, rodents are fond of nibbling the bark and twigs without any harmful effects. The best method of propagation is from the seed.

This shrub is a native of southern and western Europe. It grows mostly on dry limestone banks, requires ample light and has a better growth and greater profusion of flowers on rich soils. It is a popular ornamental in parks, being a suitable subject for planting either as a solitary specimen or in groups. Found in the Alps and mountains of southern Europe is the closely related species *L. alpinum* with hairless leaves and longer, more handsome chains of flowers.

Leaves: Alternate, trifoliate, 10—15 cm in length, with long stalks. Leaflets elliptical, with entire margin, hairy undersurface.
Flowers: Yellow, pea-like, borne in 10—20 cm-long racemes.
Fruit: Flat pods measuring about 5 cm.

1 — buds,
2 — leaves and flowers,
3 — fruits,
4 — legume with seeds

Bladder Senna

Colutea arborescens L.

Bladder senna is a 1—3 m shrub with slightly pendent shoot tips. One-year shoots are slightly angular and coloured greenish grey. The small buds are located behind the remainder of the leaf sheath. The bladder senna resembles the pea tree but can be readily distinguished by the odd number of leaflets (those of the pea tree being even). The yellow flowers are striped brownish-red at the base of the standard and have a persistent, many-pointed calyx. They appear in succession from May to June. The bladder-like seed pods, which ripen from late summer and from which the shrub takes its name, contain 30—40 kidney-shaped, markedly flattened, blackish-brown seeds, which are a good and easy means of propagation. It is recommended, however, to immerse the seeds briefly in hot water before sowing so that they will germinate uniformly.

This is a shrub of western and southern Europe. In central and western Europe its occurrence is limited to the warm, wine-growing regions. It grows in sunny positions, mostly on rocky limestone banks. It requires ample light, stands up well to dry spells but is greatly damaged by frost in severe winters. Game animals are fond of nibbling the bark.

Leaves: Alternate, pinnate, 6—15 cm long, composed of 7—13 obovate, 1—2 cm leaflets with entire margins.
Flowers: Yellow, pea-like, 2—6 on a single stalk.
Fruit: Bladder-like pods, 4—5 cm long.

1 — buds,
2 — flowers,
3 — leaves and fruits,
4 — legume with seeds

Common Box

Buxus sempervirens L.

Buxaceae

The common box is a broad shrub or small tree 4—8 m high. The twigs are square in cross section and covered with dense foliage. The inconspicuous blossoms appear in April. The female flower is situated in the centre of the cluster of male flowers. The woody capsules ripen in autumn, when they split and eject several glossy black seeds. It is a slow-growing plant but may live to an age of several hundred years. It produces abundant sprouts and stands up well to pruning.

This shrub is a native of the area bordering the Mediterranean, growing from Algeria to Greece and Asia Minor. Northward its distribution extends beyond the Alps to Alsace and some experts believe it is also native in southern England. It is found in drier, mixed broadleaved woods especially on chalk and limestone. It is a popular evergreen for shaded sections of parks and because it stands up well to pruning is also used in clipped hedges and topiary. It is reliably propagated by cuttings in late summer. The wood is the heaviest and hardest of European woods and is used in wood carving and for inlay as a substitute for ivory; it is also used in industry to make shuttles for textile looms.

Leaves: Opposite, evergreen, leathery, longish ovate, measuring 1—2 cm, dark green above, yellow-green below, with entire margins.
Flowers: Unisexual, yellowish, borne in clusters in the axils of the leaves.
Fruit: Three-pointed, 1 cm-large capsules.

1 — flower buds,
2 — flowers,
3 — leaves,
4 — fruit,
5 — seed

Bladdernut

Staphyleaceae

Staphylea pinnata L.

The bladdernut is an upright, tree-like shrub, 2—5 m high. The bark covering the stem is greenish brown with whitish longitudinal stripes. The shoots are stout and green with paired green buds at the tip of the twig, as a rule, covered with a single fused pair of scales. The whitish, drooping flowers, 5—12 cm long, appear in May—June, the round bladder-like fruits, measuring 2—3 cm, ripen at the end of September and beginning of October. They are 2- or 3-valved, with each compartment containing a single, light brown, hard, round seed the size of a pea. At one time the seeds were used to make rosaries.

Its range of natural distribution embraces central and southern Europe, extending eastward as far as the Caucasus. It grows in broadleaved forests in hilly country in moist locations with good, lime-rich soil. Nowadays it is comparatively rare in the wild, being found more frequently in parks. It is best propagated by means of seeds, which as a rule do not germinate until the second year. The bladdernut has attractive foliage as well as flowers. It thrives in sun or partial shade.

Leaves: Opposite, pinnate, composed of 5—7 leaflets; leaflets ovate, measuring 5—9 cm with finely serrate margin, the terminal leaflet petioled.
Flowers: White or pinkish, bell-shaped, borne in small drooping panicles.
Fruit: Yellow-green, inflated, rounded capsules.

1 — buds,
2 — flowers,
3 — fruits and leaves,
4 — seeds

European Spindle Tree

Euonymus europaeus L.

Celastraceae

The spindle tree is an upright shrub or small tree, 2—6 m in height. The shoots are green, tinted red on the side exposed to the sun, markedly four-angled. The buds are ovate, green, often sub-opposite. The leaf scars are whitish. The flowers are inconspicuous and appear at the end of May after the leaves. The capsules, which are 1.5 cm long, ripen in September when they split, releasing one white seed covered with an orange fleshy coat (aril) from each compartment.

This shrub's range of distribution extends northward to the Baltic Sea. It is most plentiful on moist rich soils in valleys bordering brooks, on the edges of forests, in hedgerows and in light woodlands because it is a plant that requires partial shade. It is best propagated by seeds. The leaves turn scarlet in the autumn and these, as well as the fruits, make it very attractive at this time. Farmers do not welcome its presence in the vicinity of fields because it serves as host to the black or bean aphis, which causes great damage to bean and sugar beet plantings. There are several garden varieties of which 'Albus' with white fruits, 'Red Cascade' with red fruits and 'Atropurpureus' with dull purple leaves are noteworthy.

Leaves: Opposite, elliptical to lanceolate, measuring 4—10 cm, with pointed tip and finely serrate margin. Leaf stalk short and furrowed.
Flowers: Green, tinted with red, 4-merous, measuring 5—6 mm, borne in upright clusters (dichasia).
Fruit: 4-valved reddish capsules.

1 — winter twig,
2 — flowers,
3 — leaves and fruits,
4 - seeds

Holly

Aquifoliaceae

Ilex aquifolium L.

Holly is an evergreen shrub or tree 2—10 m in height with a conical crown. The bark is smooth and grey-brown. In older trees the leaves in the upper part of the crown are only slightly spiny. The flowers, borne in the axils of the leaves, appear in May—June. The red fruits ripen in October and remain on the tree until late in the winter. In Great Britain and the United States it is used as a Christmas decoration.

A native of western and southern Europe, it thrives exceptionally well in the moist and mild coastal climate. It requires partial shade and often grows in woodland. In the Alps it is found at elevations up to 1200 m. In central Europe it is often planted in parks, though it suffers great damage by frost in severe winters. A prolific sprouter, it regenerates well and puts out new sprouts when cut back. It is a very attractive shrub in parks and is planted not only in groups but also as hedges because it can be clipped. It prefers situations sheltered from wind and winter sun and is best propagated by means of seeds. There are several good silver-and golden-leafed forms grown in gardens.

Leaves: Alternate, evergreen, ovate, 3—8 cm long, leathery, glossy green above, yellow-green below, edged with spiny teeth.
Flowers: Mostly dioecious, white and borne in clusters in the axils of the leaves.
Fruit: Bright red berry measuring 8 mm.

1 — flowers,
2 — leaves and fruits,
3 — seeds

Smoke Bush

Anacardiaceae

Cotinus coggygria SCOP.
(Syn. *Rhus cotinus* L.)

The smoke bush is a shrub or tree growing to a height of 2—8 m and forming a broad, rounded crown. The shoots are violet-brown, the buds small with pointed tips, borne in terminal clusters. The twigs when broken and leaves when crushed have a strong aromatic scent. The flowers, often dioecious, are borne in feathery panicles in June. The fruits ripen at the beginning of September. Both the flowering panicles and fruits make the smoke bush a very attractive ornamental. It produces prolific stump sprouts as well as root suckers.

The smoke bush is a native of southern Europe south of the Carpathians and of southern Siberia, its range extending to China. It grows on dry, mostly south-facing banks in thin oak and pine woods. A light-loving shrub, it stands up well to dry spells and tolerates soils containing lime and magnesium. In central and western Europe it is widely planted in parks as a specimen plant for its ornamental reddish fluffy fruiting clusters and crimson autumn foliage. It may be damaged by frost in severe winters. Propagation is by means of seeds and root cuttings. The leaves contain 20—30 per cent of quality tannins and the smoke bush is therefore cultivated on a large scale in southern areas for its yield of this substance.

Leaves: Alternate, broadly ovate to orbicular, 5—10 cm, with wedge-shaped base, long petioles, entire margin.
Flowers: Small, yellow-green, borne in dense terminal panicles.
Fruit: Heart-shaped, 3 mm, nutlets borne in plumose panicles.

1 — buds,
2 — flowers,
3 — leaves and fruits

Stag's Horn Sumach

Rhus typhina L.

Anacardiaceae

Stag's horn sumach is a shrub or small tree, 4—8 m high, often forming groups which develop from root suckers. Annual shoots are stout, rusty-brown, velvety hairy, with a prominent rust-coloured pith. The buds are small and rounded. Greenish flowers appear in June, followed by fruits ripening in October and remaining on the shrub throughout the winter. It throws out stump and root sprouts freely. Propagation is by means of seeds or root cuttings.

This shrub is a native of eastern North America from Indiana northward to Canada. It grows on rocky hillsides and dry banks, mostly on limestone. It requires abundant light but will grow on poorer and drier soils. It has been cultivated in Europe for several centuries, being valued for the vivid colouring of the foliage in the autumn and the ornamental fruits. Because of its dense root system and tendency to develop root suckers it is also sometimes planted on hillsides to prevent erosion. In some parts of Europe experiments are being carried out to cultivate it in plantations for tannin, as its leaves contain up to 25 per cent of this substance.

Leaves: Alternate, pinnate, 20—40 cm long, composed of 11—31 lanceolate leaflets with pointed tips and serrate margins.
Flowers: Dioecious, greenish-yellow, borne in dense conical panicles.
Fruit: Crimson, hairy nutlets borne in dense clusters.

1 — buds,
2 — flowers,
3 — panicle and leaves,
4 — fruit

Common Buckthorn

Rhamnus catharticus L.

The common buckthorn is a shrub or small tree growing to a height of 3—8 m with a crooked stem and asymmetric crown. The bark is blackish and in older individuals peels off in horizontal strips. The twigs are grey and terminated by a thorn between a pair of buds. The buds are blackish brown, longish and often subopposite. It is a slow-growing shrub and may live to an age of more than a hundred years. The greenish, sometimes dioecious flowers appear from May—June. The fruits ripen at the end of September; green at first, they turn black as they mature and contain four three-sided seeds which, when sown, germinate in the spring of the following year. Though it produces few shoots from cut stumps, it often throws out root suckers.

This shrub is widespread throughout most of Europe, its range extending northward to the 60th parallel and eastward to Siberia. It grows mostly on dry, sunny banks and rocky sites in hilly country. A light-loving, frost-resistant shrub, it does well even on poorer soils. The wood is hard, with brownish-red heartwood and yellow-white sapwood. The bark and fruits were used to make natural dyes and for medicinal purposes.

Leaves: Opposite, elliptical to orbicular, 3—6 cm long, with finely serrate margin and 2—4 pairs of arcuate veins.
Flowers: Inconspicuous, yellow-green, male with 4 stamens, female with four-part stigma.
Fruit: Black, 6 mm-long drupe.

1 — buds,
2 — flowers,
3 — leaves and fruits

Alder Buckthorn

Rhamnaceae

Frangula alnus MILL.
(Syn. *Rhamnus frangula* L.)

The alder buckthorn is a sparsely branched shrub or tree 3—7 m in height. When young the bark is violet-brown with whitish corky pores (lenticels); the buds have no scales but are covered with rust-felted hairs. The flowers appear successively between May and August, the fruits likewise ripening successively between July and September, turning from green to red and black. It is a fast-growing shrub attaining an age of 80 years or so.

Widespread throughout most of Europe, its range extends far to the north and eastward to Siberia. In central and western Europe it grows in abundance in damp and swampy sites in riverine woods and up to mountain elevations. It also occurs in acid oak stands and pine woods where the level of underground water is near the surface. A shrub requiring semi-shade, it is completely frost-resistant and will grow on poorer soils where it has sufficient moisture. It is propagated readily by means of seeds and throws out a profusion of stump and root suckers. Ash from the wood was at one time used to make gun powder and the bark is used in medicine.

Leaves: Alternate, broadly elliptical to obovate, 4—7 cm in length, with shortly pointed tip and entire margin.
Flowers: Small, greenish-yellow, 5-merous, borne in clusters of 3—7 in the axils of the leaves.
Fruit: Round, black drupe 6 mm in diameter.

1 — buds,
2 — flowers,
3 — leaves and fruits,
4 — seed

Tamarisk

Tamaricaceae

Tamarix gallica L.
(Syn. *Tamarix anglica* WEBB.)

Tamarisk is a thin shrub or small tree, 2—7 m high. The shoots are slender and green to reddish brown. The short terminal twigs are shed together with the leaves. The buds are small, the leaf buds slightly pointed, the flower buds round. The pink flowers are borne from June till the end of July. The capsules ripen and split in September. The seed retains its powers of germination for only a few weeks and must be sown in moist soil.

This species is widespread in southern Europe, its range extending from Spain and France as far as Asia Minor. It is naturalized near the coasts of southern England. Where native, it grows in the coastal belt, mostly in river valleys and on river terraces, and prefers light soils, also tolerating salty soils. In central and western Europe it is cultivated as an ornamental shrub in parks and gardens. It requires full sun and adequately moist soil, best of all with underground water level close to the surface. In more northerly regions it is greatly damaged by frost. Propagation is by woody, winter cuttings.

Leaves: Alternate, small (2 mm), lanceolate, pale green with translucent margins.
Flowers: Small, pink, borne in thick, cylindrical clusters 3—5 cm long.
Fruit: Capsules, 3—5 mm long, borne in cylindrical clusters.

1 — buds,
2 — flowers,
3 — leaves and fruits

Mezereon

Thymelaeaceae

Daphne mezereum L.

Mezereon is a small, sparsely branched shrub growing to a height of 30—120 cm. The twigs are greyish, the buds dark brown. The flowers appear before the leaves in early spring (February—March) and have a strong fragrance. The round drupes ripen in July and contain a single ovoid black-brown seed. Both fruit and bark are poisonous.

This shrub is widespread throughout most of Europe, where it grows in woodlands, especially beech stands. In England it occurs rarely in woods on chalk and limestone. It grows best in moist soil rich in humus and may be found in valley woods as well as mixed mountain forests, occasionally also in subalpine meadows. It requires semi-shade and will not thrive in sunny aspects. It is a popular ornamental shrub for the rock garden and therefore often taken up in the wild and transplanted to private gardens. For this reason many countries have proclaimed it a protected species and digging it up in the wild an offence punishable by law. It is readily propagated by means of seeds.

Growing on dry and warm banks in central and western Europe is the related species *D. cneorum*, a dwarf shrub about 30 cm in height, of sprawling habit with evergreen, leathery leaves and fragrant red flowers.

Leaves: Deciduous, alternate, borne in terminal clusters, lanceolate, with entire margin and pale grey-green undersurface.
Flowers: Pinkish red, trumpet-shaped, borne in groups of 3 above the leaf scar.
Fruit: Round, red, sessile berry, 8 mm in diameter.

1 — buds,
2 — flowers,
3 — leaves and fruits,
4 — seed

Sea Buckthorn

Hippophae rhamnoides L.

Elaeagnaceae

Sea buckthorn is a spiny shrub or small crooked tree 2—7 m high. The stem is covered with reddish-brown bark breaking up into scales. Annual shoots are golden brown and terminate in a spine; the flower buds of male plants are round, those of female plants small. The flowers appear in April. The orange-coloured fruits ripen at the end of September and remain on the plant late into the winter as they are only taken by birds when other fruits have been finished. This shrub has a wide-spreading root system and puts out root suckers, and is thereby a good plant for anchoring sand dunes. The roots have nodules containing nitrogen-fixing bacteria that enrich both shrub and soil with this important substance. The sea buckthorn is reliably propagated by means of seeds and root cuttings.

A native of southern and western Europe, it grows on coastal dunes as far north as Poland, Sweden and Norway. It is found mainly on gravelly and sandy deposits formed by streams and rivers and on sand dunes bordering the sea. It is a sun-loving species that does well even in poorer soils. It is planted in parks as an ornamental because of its attractive fruits; however, shrubs of both sexes must be close to one another to produce these.

Leaves: Alternate, narrowly lanceolate, 4—7 cm long and only 5—8 mm wide, green above and silvery-grey felted below, with entire margins.
Flowers: Dioecious, insignificant, greenish, borne in clusters.
Fruit: Ovate, orange-coloured berries measuring 8 mm.

1 — buds,
2 — ♂ flower buds,
3 — ♀ flowers,
4 — ♂ flowers,
5 — leaves and fruits

English Ivy

Hedera helix L.

Ivy is an evergreen climber that either creeps along the ground or climbs up rocks, trees and walls, to which it holds fast with its roots. However, it is by no means a parasite and takes neither water nor nutrients from the host plant. It may live to an age of several hundred years, the stem becoming up to 20 cm thick. Unlike other European trees and shrubs it bears flowers at the beginning of October, and the fruits ripen the following spring, in March. The berries contain 3—5 pale, furrowed seeds, which are dispersed in the droppings of birds.

It is a native of western, central and southern Europe, its range extending eastward to Asia Minor and Caucasia in continental Europe. It is found mainly in beech woods, where it grows on stony, calcareous soils or ones rich in humus; in Britain it will grow almost anywhere. Ideal for its growth are the mild winters of the coastal climate and moist air. It tolerates strong shade but bears flowers and fruits only if supplied with adequate light. It is used in parks to form a green carpet in shaded spots where turf will not thrive, and to cover walls and rocks. Propagation is by means of cuttings and seeds.

Leaves: Opposite, persistent, leathery, longish ovate on the fruiting twigs and 3—5-lobed with heart-shaped base on the remaining shoots.
Flowers: Yellow-green, 5-merous, borne in umbels.
Fruit: Blue-black, round berries, 6 mm in diameter.

1 — leaves,
2 — fruit-bearing twig with leaves and flowers,
3 — fruits

Cornelian Cherry

Cornus mas L.

The cornelian cherry is a shrub or small tree with a thin but widespreading crown growing to a height of 3—7 m. The yellow-brown bark on older shoots breaks up into scales. One-year shoots are slender, erect, green or tinged with violet. The leaf buds are lanceolate, opposite, and stand out slightly from the twig. The flower buds are round (the size of a pea) and easily distinguished from the leaf buds. The flowers appear before the leaves in March. The fruits ripen in September; they are edible but turn sweet only after the first frost. Inside the pulp is a hard, elongate seed which, when sown, does not germinate until the second year.

This is a warmth-loving species growing mostly in southern Europe and Asia Minor. In central Europe it exists as a relic of the warm period following the Ice Age, growing in warm, mainly limestone situations. It occurs on sunny and rocky banks or in oak stands. It thrives quite well in dry locations but requires lighter soil rich in humus. It is planted in parks for its early flowers and attractive red fruits. Propagation is by means of seeds, summer cuttings and root suckers. The wood is very hard, with reddish-brown heartwood.

Leaves: Opposite, ovate with attenuated point, 4—9 cm long, with entire margin and 3—4 pairs of curved veins.
Flowers: Small, yellow, 4-merous, borne in round umbels.
Fruit: Carmine red, barrel-shaped drupes measuring 1.5—2 cm.

1 — buds,
2 — flowers,
3 — leaves and fruits,
4 — seed

White Dogwood

Cornus alba L.
(Syn. *Cornus tatarica* MILL.)

The white dogwood is a widespreading, sparsely branched shrub with drooping twigs, growing to a height of 2—3 m. The twigs are bright red, in more heavily shaded locations yellow. The buds resemble those of the red dogwood, but are somewhat larger and more tomentose. The white flowers appear in May and June, the fruits ripen in September. The hard seed is flattened, ovate.

This shrub is a native of eastern Europe and Siberia, its range extending eastward to northern China and Korea. In this area it grows mainly in the valleys of large rivers, where it can be one of the main species in the shrub layer of riverine woods. In central and western Europe it is planted in parks as a shrub beneath groups of trees. Both the red twigs and white fruits are very ornamental. A completely frost-resistant species, it tolerates shade and the smoke-laden atmosphere of large cities. Propagation is by suckers and cuttings. Also planted in parks is the closely related species *Cornus stolonifera* Michx. (*C. sericea*. L.) of America, which is readily propagated by means of the drooping branches which take root easily. This dogwood has white flowers and small, round, white drupes containing a single, hard, ribbed seed.

Leaves: Opposite, elliptical, pointed at the apex, 5—10 cm long, with entire margin, 4—6 pairs of curved veins and blue-green undersurface.
Flowers: White, 4-merous, borne in flat terminal heads (cymes).
Fruit: Round, white drupes, 7 mm in diameter.

1 — buds,
2 — flowers,
3 — leaves and fruits,
4 — seed

Red Dogwood

Cornaceae

Cornus sanguinea L.

The red dogwood is a shrub growing to a height of 3—5 m. One-year shoots are purplish-red on the side exposed to the sun and green on the shaded side. The buds are flat and appressed. The white flowers appear at the end of May and the fruits ripen in September. It sprouts freely from stumps and roots. It is best propagated by means of seeds; these, however, do not germinate until the spring of the second year.

It is widespread throughout western, central and eastern Europe. It stands up well to strong shade and forms the lower shrub storey in riverine woods and mixed broad-leaved forests in hilly country. Though it generally grows on fresh to moist soils it thrives quite well in dry soils and in England can form dense scrub on chalk; it also occurs widely in hedges. Because of its wide-spreading root system and profusion of root suckers it is sometimes planted on steep banks to hold the soil. Propagation is by means of seeds and root cuttings. The leaves turn a bright red in autumn. The wood is hard and reddish.

Leaves: Opposite, broadly elliptical, 4—8 cm large, with shortly pointed apex, entire margin and 3—4 pairs of arcuate veins.
Flowers: White, 4-merous, borne in flat terminal cymes.
Fruit: Blue-black, 6 mm-long drupe with round, hard seed.

1 — buds,
2 — flowers,
3 — leaves and fruits,
4 — seed

Alpenrose

Rhododendron hirsutum L.

Alpenrose is a densely branched, evergreen shrub growing to a height of 0.4—1 m. The glowing flowers appear in June and July. The capsules ripen and split at the end of September.

This shrub is a native of the Alps, mainly the eastern part, its range extending westward only to Switzerland. It grows from 1200—2500 m in open woodlands and the dwarf pine belt. It is more plentiful on limestone and dolomite slopes. It is a popular shrub for rock gardens, parks and gardens. Also found in the Alps is the closely related species *Rhododendron ferrugineum* L., which grows farther west, to the French Alps and the Pyrenees, and unlike *R. hirsutum* has no preference for calcareous soils, growing above the tree line in stands of dwarf pine on siliceous soil. It attains a height of 1 m; the leaves are densely covered with rust-coloured hairs below and the flowers are a darker, pinkish red. When planted in gardens both these rhododendrons should be provided with a moist soil rich in humus. The large-flowered and taller species, 2—4 m high, developed by the crossing of American and Chinese rhododendrons, are generally cultivated in parks and gardens.

Leaves: Alternate, evergreen, longish elliptical, leathery, 1—3 cm long, pubescent below.
Flowers: Pink, bell-shaped, 5-pointed, borne in clusters of 3—10, the stalk and calyx hairy.
Fruit: 5-valved capsules containing small seeds.

1 — flowers and leaves,
2 — underside of leaves,
3 — large-flowered hybrid

Common Privet

Ligustrum vulgare L.

Oleaceae

The common privet is an upright, densely branched shrub 1—4 m high. One-year shoots are erect, arching and grey. The brown, ovate buds are often subopposite and are borne on prominent peg-like projections. The white flowers appear in June. The fruits ripen in September and remain on the shrub until late in winter.

This species is widespread in southern, central, western and eastern Europe, extending north to the Baltic Sea. It thrives well on rich, calcareous soils and is most abundant in lowlands in the valleys of rivers and streams though it is also found in the foothills up to heights of 600—700 m. It appears to thrive quite well even in drier soils as evidenced by its occurrence in drier situations in oak stands. A shade-tolerant species, it is found not only on the edges of woods and in hedgerows, but also in mixed broadleaved woods. It is readily propagated by means of seeds and winter cuttings. Because it stands up well to clipping, *L. vulgare* is a popular plant for hedges growing up to 2 m high, but, once widely used, has now been almost completely replaced for this purpose by the Japanese privet, *L. ovalifolium*. In parks it is planted in shrubbery borders and as a shrub layer beneath groups of trees.

Leaves: Opposite, lanceolate, 3—6 cm long, slightly leathery, dark green, with entire margin.
Flowers: White, 4-merous, grouped in upright, terminal, racemose panicles.
Fruits: Round, black berries, 7 mm in diameter, containing 2 seeds.

1 — buds,
2 — flowers,
3 — leaves and fruits,
4 — seed

Lilac

Oleaceae

Syringa vulgaris L.

Lilac is a large shrub or small tree growing to a height of 2—6 m. The bark is grey-brown, breaking up into longitudinal strips that peel with age. The shoots are slender, upright and olive green; the ovate buds are covered by several scales. The highly fragrant flowers appear at the beginning of May. The fruits ripen in September and remain on the bush until the spring of the following year. The capsules contain 2 winged seeds. This is a quick-growing shrub and produces stump and root suckers freely.

It is a native of the Balkan Peninsula, mainly Bulgaria and Yugoslavia, where it grows mostly on rocky, limestone slopes up to more than 1000 m. In central and western Europe it is very popular as an ornamental shrub and is widely cultivated in parks and gardens. Many cultivated varieties are grown with flowers ranging in colour from white to red and violet; these are often grafted onto privet. Lilac is frequently found more or less naturalized in hedges, on banks and the edges of woods especially near built-up areas.

Leaves: Opposite, heart-shaped, tapering to a point at the apex, 6—10 cm long, semi-leathery, with entire margin.
Flowers: Trumpet-shaped, violet-pink, borne in pyramidal clusters 10—20 cm long.
Fruit: Two-valved, flattened capsules 1 cm long.

1 — buds,
2 — leaves and flowers,
3 — fruits

Forsythia or Golden Bell

Oleaceae

Forsythia suspensa [THUNB.] VAHL.

Forsythia is a broad shrub with arching pendent branches reaching a height of 3 m. The shoots appear four-angled and are hollow. The elliptical buds are opposite. The golden yellow flowers appear in March and April before the leaves unfold. The capsules ripen and split to release the small winged seeds in September.

This shrub is a native of northern and central China, where it grows on mountain slopes, and was introduced into the parks and gardens of western and central Europe almost 150 years ago. It is very popular for the abundance and brightness of its blooms as well as for its early flowering season. It is planted either as a solitary specimen, in groups or as a border plant alongside paths. It requires full sun if it is to bear a rich profusion of flowers and is moderate in its demands on soil moisture. It is slightly sensitive to frost and its shoots are damaged by frost in severe winters. Propagation is by means of seeds and summer cuttings. Also widely cultivated in European parks is *F. viridissima*, with simple leaves, likewise a native of China. Cross-breeding of the two above species produced the hybrid x *F. intermedia* with simple and occasionally trifoliate leaves. This hybrid and its named forms, notably 'Spectabilis' and 'Lynwood' are commonly met with in gardens.

Leaves: Opposite, trifoliate or trilobed on stout shoots, simple on old twigs, ovate, 6—9 cm long, with serrate margins.
Flowers: Golden yellow, bell-shaped, borne in clusters of 1—3.
Fruit: 2-valved, flat capsules measuring 1.5 cm.

1 — buds,
2 — flowers,
3 — leaves,
4 — fruits

The Duke of Argyll's Tea Tree

Solanaceae

Lycium halimifolium L.
(Syn. *Lycium barbarum* AIT.)

The Duke of Argyll's tea tree is a thorny shrub, 1—2 m in height, with long, drooping pale grey shoots. Older twigs have short side twigs terminated by a thorn. The small buds are borne on broad, peg-like projections. The purplish flowers appear in succession from May to June and the fruits ripen in September. The berries contain a large number of lentil-like seeds about 2 mm across. The plant is readily propagated by means of seeds or division as well as summer and winter cuttings.

This shrub is widespread in southern Europe, where it grows mostly in the coastal areas on dry banks. In central and western Europe it is planted for its foliage and to prevent erosion on dry, steep banks. It does very well in dry sites and in warmer regions is sufficiently frost-resistant. It multiplies by producing root suckers. The fruits are eaten by birds and the seeds dispersed by them over a wide area so that in central and western Europe it is frequently naturalized.

Leaves: Alternate, lanceolate, 2—5 cm long, broadest in the bottom half, grey-green, with entire margin.
Flowers: Pinkish violet, trumpet-shaped, located in the axils of the leaves.
Fruit: Egg-shaped, scarlet berry, 1—1.5 cm in diameter, with green calyx.

1 — buds,
2 — flowers,
3 — leaves and fruits,
4 — seeds

Common Elder

Caprifoliaceae

Sambucus nigra L.

Common elder is a large shrub or small tree up to 10 m high, developing a broad crown and stem up to 30 cm in diameter. The pale grey bark becomes deeply furrowed and corky with age. The shoots are stout, grey, slightly angular in cross section and covered with numerous white corky pores. The opposite, ovate and semi-naked buds are located above a large leaf scar shaped like a half-moon. The white flower clusters, 12 to 20 cm across, appear in June; the fruits ripen in September.

Widespread throughout most of Europe, extending north to Scotland, Sweden and Norway, it occurs in lowland and hilly country up to elevations of 600 m, mostly on soils rich in humus, i.e. at the edges of woods, in clearings, waste dumps and in the vicinity of human dwellings. It can thrive in heavy shade and thus is often found growing also in forest stands, where it frequently becomes a weed difficult to eradicate. It grows rapidly on moist, rich soils, sprouts readily from stumps and multiplies from the seed which is dispersed by birds. At one time it was extensively planted alongside country dwellings, and its flowers, fruits and seeds were used as drugs for home remedies and for wine making.

Leaves: Opposite, pinnate, composed of 5—7 ovate leaflets, 10—12 cm in length with serrate margins; the terminal leaflet is larger than the others.
Flowers: Small, yellowish-white, borne in broad, flat heads.
Fruit: Round, black berries, 5 mm in diameter, borne in broad heads.

1 — buds,
2 — flowers,
3 — leaves and fruits,
4 — seed

Red or Scarlet-berried Elder

Caprifoliaceae

Sambucus racemosa L.

The red elder is a shrub or small tree, 1—4 m in height. The twigs are stout, grey-brown, with a broad circle of rust-coloured pith in cross section. The round buds, about 1 cm across, are arranged opposite each other on the twig, which is usually terminated by two buds. The yellowish flowers appear in April and May; the fruits ripen in July and August. It has a widespreading root system and increases also by root suckers.

This shrub is widespread throughout most of Europe, extending farther north and growing higher up in the mountains than the common elder, sometimes as high as the tree line. On the other hand, it is rarely found at elevations below 300 m in central Europe and is not native to Britain, though it is sometimes naturalized. It grows in similar places to the common elder, i.e. mostly on soils rich in humus and nitrogen. It is an important pioneer in the colonizing of logged areas or ones damaged by natural catastrophes. Its seeds are dispersed in such places mostly by birds of the thrush tribe, which are fond of the fruits. It is planted as an ornamental shrub in parks for its attractive flowers and red fruits; however, it requires greater soil moisture in such locations. Propagation is by hardwood cuttings and seeds.

Leaves: Opposite, pinnate, composed of 5—7 ovate lanceolate leaflets, 10 cm long, with serrate margin and long attenuated point at the apex.
Flowers: Small, greenish-yellow, borne in ovate panicles.
Fruit: Round, red berries, 4 mm in diameter.

1 — buds,
2 — flowers,
3 — leaves and fruits,
4 — seed

Wayfaring Tree

Viburnum lantana L.

The wayfaring tree is a shrub of upright habit, 1 to 4 m high. One-year shoots are straight, grey-felted, older twigs are yellow-brown. The buds are opposite, naked, white-felted. Leaf buds are the folded felted incipient leaves; flower buds, 2 cm across, are semi-spherical, borne at the tips of the shoots. The whitish flowers appear in May and June succeeded by the fruits, which change colour from green to red and black as they ripen, being fully ripe at the end of September or beginning of October and remaining on the shrub until winter. The wayfaring tree has a fairly rapid growth and produces stump sprouts freely.

Its chief area of distribution is southern Europe, but it also grows in warm situations in central and western Europe reaching southern England. It is found mainly on warm, sunny banks in hilly country, where it occurs in thickets at the edges of woods and in open oak stands. On limestone substrates it is also found in the mountains up to elevations above 1000 m. The red-black ripening fruit and felted foliage are very attractive and for that reason the wayfaring tree is also planted in parks.

Leaves: Opposite, elliptical, 7—10 cm long, with serrate margin, grey-green felted undersurface and prominent venation.

Flowers: Small, white, 5-merous, borne in rounded cymes.

Fruit: Black, flattened, 8 mm drupe, containing a single, furrowed stone.

1 — buds,
2 — flower buds,
3 — flowers,
4 — leaves and fruits,
5 — seed

Viburnum rhytidophyllum HEMSL.

Caprifoliaceae

Viburnum rhytidophyllum is an evergreen shrub of upright habit growing to a height of 2—3 m. The shoots are yellowish tomentose. The clusters of flowers begin to develop in autumn, remain dormant through the winter and unfold during May and June. The fruits ripen at the end of September.

This species is a native of central and western China and was introduced into Europe as an ornamental at the end of the nineteenth century, nowadays being planted in the parks of central and western Europe. The large leaves are very decorative and remain on the shrub throughout the winter, thus augmenting the poor selection of European evergreens in parks. It is a suitable subject for a tall green screen, green backdrop and for filling in odd spaces, for it tolerates moderate shade. During severe winters the foliage can be damaged by frost. Another evergreen species cultivated in Europe is *Viburnum utile*, likewise of China, which grows only to a height of 1.5 m, has 3—6 cm-long elliptical leaves and bears clusters of white flowers in April. It is one parent of the popular garden hybrid *V.* x *burkwoodii*, which bears strongly fragrant, pink-budded, white waxy blooms from February to May.

Leaves: Opposite, evergreen, elliptic to narrowly oblong, 9—18 cm long, dark green, corrugated, with grey-felted undersurface and finely toothed margin.
Flowers: Small, yellow-white, borne in 15 cm wide clusters.
Fruit: Black, flattened drupe.

1 — flowers,
2 — leaves and fruits

Guelder Rose

Caprifoliaceae

Viburnum opulus L.

The guelder rose is a shrub, 2—4 m in height, of upright habit with yellowish bark. The shoots are yellow-grey, faintly angular in cross section, the buds ovate, reddish brown, with short stalks. The whitish flowers appear in May and June followed by the fruits, which develop only from the small flowers in the centre of the cluster. When the small red berries ripen in September the pulp has an unpleasant smell; enclosed inside is a flat, pinkish stone. The guelder rose is a fast-growing shrub with widespreading root system which produces both stump and root suckers freely. It is best propagated by means of seeds and hard- and softwood cuttings.

Widely distributed throughout most of Europe, it extends northward even beyond the Arctic Circle. In central and western Europe it grows in damp situations alongside streams and rivers, being particularly fond of soil rich in humus and lime. Since it thrives well in shade it is often found in woods and scrub. It is most plentiful in lowland and hilly country, individual specimens occurring in the mountains up to about 1000 m.

Also widely planted in parks is the cultivated, double-flowered variety *V. o.* 'Sterile', the snowball tree, which produces round clusters of white flowers, all of which are sterile.

Leaves: 3—5-lobed, opposite, 6—9 cm long, with coarsely serrate margin and several round glands on the leaf stalk.
Flowers: White, borne in an umbel-shaped cyme; the sterile, peripheral flowers are large, the others small.
Fruit: Red, 8 mm drupe.

1 — buds,
2 — leaves and flowers,
3 — fruits,
4 — seed

Fly Honeysuckle

Lonicera xylosteum L.

Caprifoliaceae

Fly honeysuckle is a densely branched shrub growing to a height of 1—2 m. The twigs are grey, hollow inside, the buds longish ovate with pointed tip, placed almost at right angles to the twig. Immediately above the pair of buds there is usually another pair of smaller ones. The whitish flowers appear in May. The red berries ripen at the end of July. They are bitter and inedible but not poisonous. This honeysuckle is a fast-growing shrub that can be propagated by means of seeds as well as by woody and green cuttings.

This shrub is widespread throughout most of Europe, its range extending far east to Siberia. In central and western Europe it grows on the edges and in the shrub layer of woods, on scrub-covered banks and in hedgerows. It likes fresh, rich soil and tolerates fairly heavy shade. It is most plentiful in hilly country but also grows in the mountains up to elevations of 1000 m. It is frequently planted in parks and gardens as a hedge plant because it stands up well to clipping and is covered with foliage early in spring. More commonly planted in parks, however, is the taller species *L. tatarica* of Siberia, with pink flowers and bright red berries.

Leaves: Opposite, broadly elliptical, tapering to a short point at the apex, 3—6 cm long, pubescent, with entire margin.
Flowers: Yellow-white, growing in pairs on a single, downy stalk.
Fruit: Bright red berries, 7 mm across, two on one stalk.

1 — buds,
2 — flowers,
3 — leaves and fruits

Black Honeysuckle

Lonicera nigra L.

The black honeysuckle is a sparsely branched shrub of upright habit, growing to 1—2 m in height. The shoots are slender, often curved, the buds opposite, with pointed tips, standing out from the twig at an angle. The flowers appear in May and June. The black berries ripen in August; they are inedible and cause vomiting when eaten. Propagation is by means of seeds as well as by summer and winter cuttings.

This is a shrub of the central European mountains, mostly the Alps, Sudetens and Carpathians. Even there, however, it is comparatively scarce, growing mainly on rocky banks, in clearings and on soils rich in humus alongside streams, at elevations between 600 and 1500 m. It is entirely frost-resistant and tolerates heavy shade. Also found in mountain areas are the species *Lonicera alpigena* and *Lonicera coerulea*, both of which grow at higher elevations between 1000 and 2000 m, mostly on light, lime-rich soils. They produce flowers in May. The first species has greenish flowers succeeded by glossy red, paired berries, the second yellowish flowers and large, blue-black berries produced by the fusion of two ovaries.

Leaves: Opposite, longish elliptical, 4—6 cm long, with bluntly pointed apex, entire margin, blue-green undersurface.
Flowers: Dull red, borne in pairs on a smooth stalk.
Fruit: Black berries, 8 mm in diameter, paired on one stalk.

1 — buds,
2 — leaves and flowers,
3 — fruits

Perfoliate Honeysuckle

Lonicera caprifolium L.

The perfoliate honeysuckle is a stem-twining, climbing shrub growing to a height of several metres. The light brown bark on the stem peels off in long, longitudinal strips. The twigs are slender and hollow, the buds opposite, ovate, with pointed tips. The long flowers appear at the end of May and emit a strong fragrance, especially in the evening. The red fruits ripen from August onwards and are soon dispersed by birds.

Widespread mostly in southern Europe, it extends north to southern Germany and the warmer regions of Czechoslovakia, growing there at the edges of forests, in thickets and in open broadleaved woods. It is a popular shrub in parks and gardens, where it is planted as an ornamental climber on archways, fences, pergolas and the walls of buildings. Not only does it have lovely fragrant blossoms but also attractive red fruits. To bear a profusion of flowers, however, it requires a sunny and warm situation. It is readily propagated by means of seeds as well as by cuttings. It is hardier than the common honeysuckle *(L. periclymenum)*. Crossed with the related species *L. etrusca*, it yielded the hybrid x *L. americana* with striking purple flowers.

Leaves: Opposite, with entire margin, the top ones pairing to form a single round to oval leaf, the bottom pairs ovate and fused only at the base.
Flowers: Tubular, pinkish-white to yellow, borne in groups of 6 in the axils of the leaves.
Fruit: Red, round berries.

1 — buds,
2 — leaves and flowers,
3 — fruits

Honeysuckle or Woodbine

Caprifoliaceae

Lonicera periclymenum L.

Honeysuckle is a stem-twining, vigorous climber growing to a length of 5—8 m and sometimes to an age of 50 years, when it develops a thicker stem. The twining stem is capable of choking and even strangling weaker trees. The shoots are yellowish to reddish, the buds opposite, standing out from the twig at an angle. Beneath the buds is a clearly discernible leaf scar. The attractive, fragrant flowers appear in June and July, the fruits ripen in September and October.

This shrub is widespread in southern and western Europe, its range extending as far as northern Africa and Asia Minor. In western Europe it is most plentiful on fertile soils in riverine woods, also occurring on shrub-covered banks and at the edges of forests. It bears a great profusion of flowers if provided with abundant light, but tolerates partial shade. It requires warmth and the shoots are easily damaged by frost. It is widely cultivated as a vigorous, ornamental climber in parks and gardens, where it is used to cover fences, walls and pergolas. Propagation is by means of seeds and cuttings. The variety *serotina* has dark red flowers.

Leaves: Opposite, ovate elliptical, 4—6 cm long, never fused, with entire margins and blue-green undersurface.
Flowers: Tubular, yellow-white, 4—6 cm long, clustered at the end of the twig.
Fruit: Red berries borne in clusters of 10—16.

1 — buds,
2 — flowers,
3 — leaves and fruits,
4 — seeds

Snowberry

Caprifoliaceae

Symphoricarpos albus BLACKE

Snowberry is a densely branched shrub 1—2 m in height. The twigs are slender, yellow-brown, with small, ovate, opposite buds. The small flowers appear in succession from June to August followed by white berries, which likewise ripen successively from August to October. This shrub is an important source of food for bees, providing them with nourishment in the summer months when most woody plants have already ceased flowering.

The snowberry is a native of North America, where it grows on dry and stony banks from the Atlantic to the Pacific coast. It was introduced into Europe in the second half of the nineteenth century and is now a common shrub there, becoming well naturalized in many places. It is planted to form hedges, prevent erosion on steep banks and for its foliage and in non-fertile areas is valued because of its moderate requirements on soil fertility and moisture. It sprouts prolifically from stumps and also produces root suckers freely so that in parks it sometimes spreads to such an extent that it becomes a weed difficult to eradicate. It is readily propagated by means of cuttings and root suckers.

Leaves: Opposite, broadly ovate, 2—5 cm long, with entire margins; on vigorous shoots the leaves are asymmetrically lobed.
Flowers: Bell-shaped, small, pinkish, borne in terminal spikes.
Fruit: Round, white berries about 1 cm in diameter.

1 — buds,
2 — leaves and flowers,
3 — fruits,
4 — seed

SHRUBS IN GARDENS
AND HOUSING DEVELOPMENTS

Today the trend is to make gardens and the open spaces between blocks of apartment houses an extension of man's living
space. Vegetables and fruit trees are being replaced in large
part by terraces, lawns, pools and ornamental shrubs. Because
gardens and the open spaces between apartment blocks are far
smaller than public parks, smaller trees and above all shrubs
are being widely used.

In order to create a suitable environment for a restful and
undisturbed hour of sipping coffee or tea, reading a book or
pursuing some other quiet pastime the garden must be isolated
both optically and acoustically from the surroundings and
street traffic. It is just as important to conceal disruptive and
unattractive elements such as a wire fence, wall or shed, and in
this man is superbly aided by shrubs which can be used to form
a green partition, either as a trimmed hedge or freely growing
border of green. Best suited for hedges are densely-branched
shrubs which stand up well to pruning. Impenetrable thorny
species can be used in places where exceptionally good shelter
is desired. The choice of shrubs for a freely-growing border
includes most species and is governed by the quality of the soil
of the given site, the abundance of light and the required height
of the border. The aesthetic aspect is likewise not to be over-
looked, the decisive factors here being the flowers and fruit
borne by the given shrubs.

Many shrubs bear an abundance of beautiful and fragrant
flowers or ornamental fruits and are thus an important decorative element in the garden, able, in many cases, to serve the
same purpose as annual and perennial flowers. Native shrubs,
their ornamental forms and above all related and established
exotic species offer a wide selection from which to choose those

suited for various sites and locations and for various purposes. Besides the standard shrubs from 1 to 3 m high, there are small or dwarf sorts of up to only 40—60 cm, especially well suited for the rock or heath garden. There are also shrubs that are practically small trees with their height of 5—7 m.

As to the flowering period, some shrubs bear blossoms before the onset of spring with the last remnants of snow still lying about, whereas others flower late, opening their blooms just before or after the leaves fall. The colour of the flowers is another important aspect and the choice is wide, ranging from white through yellow, pink, red, and blue to violet. Size also is variable, ranging from the practically indiscernible greenish blooms of *Hippophae rhamnoides* to the large showy flowers of *Magnolia* and *Rhododendron*. Other shrubs with unobtrusive flowers are loveliest in the autumn, when they are covered with bright ornamental fruits — *Cotoneaster*, *Pyracantha*, *Hippophae*, etc.

Just as important as the choice of shrubs is their location and planting in the garden; here are a few hints on these points. Unless it is desired to plant a hedge or green barrier or unless the garden is a formal one laid out in a geometrical pattern, shrubs should never be planted in straight rows. They are best set out in small irregular groups of 3—5 or more, depending on ultimate size. Shrubs that are exceptionally attractive because of their habit of growth, flowers or fruits should be planted as solitary specimens in the turf or in front of a hedge of evergreen or deciduous shrubs (*Exochorda*, *Cotinus*, *Cotoneaster*, *Viburnum carlesii*, etc.).

The best time to plant deciduous shrubs is in the autumn after they have shed their leaves. Evergreen shrubs, like conifers, are best planted in spring just before they begin to put out new shoots. They are usually transplanted with the roots encased in a ball of earth. To make sure that the transplanted shrub becomes well established and grows well it is important to preserve the ratio between the top and underground parts. When lifting a shrub its roots are often damaged quite severely and diminished in size and therefore it is necessary to cut back the top parts accordingly. Long and damaged roots should be shortened and with top growth it is necessary to remove weak shoots and cut back the thicker ones. This should always be done with a sharp knife or secateurs so that the cut is clean and smooth. The top growth of evergreen shrubs planted out with a ball of earth is not cut back. To ensure that the shrub will become well established it is advisable to add peat, compost, or well decayed manure and to water well after planting.

If shrubs are to grow well and produce an abundance of flowers it is necessary to keep in mind their requirements. Sun-loving shrubs should have plenty of light. Shade-loving species should not be planted in a spot exposed to full sunlight. Shrubs that like moisture will need damp locations and those that need drier conditions must have a really well-drained site. The result will be healthy and vigorous shrubs requiring the minimum of work and providing a feast for the eyes.

Table I. List of Shrubs According to Height, Showing Suitability for Hedges and Different Situations

Height	Shrub	Hedge	Sunny Places	Semi-shaded Places	Shady Places
5—7 m	Caragana arborescens	+	+	+	
	Cornus florida		+	+	
	Cornus mas		+	+	
	Corylus avellana	+	+	+	
	Crataegus laevigata (oxyacantha)	+		+	+
	Hippophae rhamnoides		+		
	Ilex aquifolium			+	+
	Rhamnus cathartica		+	+	
	Sambucus nigra			+	+
3—4 m	Cornus sanguinea	+		+	+
	Cotinus coggygria		+		
	Cydonia oblonga		+	+	
	Laburnum anagyroides		+	+	
	Mespilus germanica		+	+	
	Philadelphus coronarius	+	+	+	
	Rhamnus frangula			+	+
	Rhus typhina		+	+	
	Sambucus racemosa		+	+	
	Staphylea pinnata			+	
	Syringa vulgaris	+	+	+	
	Viburnum opulus		+	+	
	Viburnum rhytidophyllum		+	+	
2—3 m	Amelanchier ovalis		+		
	Berberis vulgaris	+	+	+	
	Buxus sempervirens	+		+	+
	Colutea arborescens		+	+	
	Cotoneaster multiflora		+		
	Deutzia scabra	+		+	
	Euonymus europaea			+	+
	Exochorda racemosa		+	+	

Table I. (continued)

Height	Shrub	Hedge	Sunny Places	Semi-shaded Places	Shady Places
	Forsythia suspensa		+	+	
	Ligustrum vulgare	+		+	+
	Lonicera tatarica	+		+	+
	Prunus spinosa	+	+	+	
	Pyracantha coccinea	+	+	+	
	Ribes alpinum	+		+	
	Rosa canina	+	+		
	Spiraea salicifolia	+	+	+	
	Tamarix gallica		+		
	Viburnum lantana	+	+	+	
1—2 m	Berberis thunbergii	+	+		
	Chaenomeles lagenaria		+		
	Lycium halimifolium		+	+	
	Rhododendron sp.			+	+
	Ribes sanguineum		+		
	Rosa rugosa	+	+		
	Sarothamnus scoparius		+		
	Spiraea × vanhouttei	+	+	+	
	Symphoricarpos albus	+	+	+	
	Viburnum carlesii		+	+	
	Weigela florida		+	+	
1-1.5 m	Chaenomeles japonica		+		
	Cotoneaster horizontalis		+		
	Cytisus purpureus		+	+	
	Daphne mezereum			+	+
	Mahonia aquifolium	+		+	+
	Potentilla fruticosa	+	+		
	Ribes grossularia	+	+		
	Spiraea japonica	+	+	+	
	Spiraea thunbergii		+		

Table II. List of Shrubs According to Their Flowering Period

Flowering Period	Shrub	
Early-flowering from late February (II) to mid-May (V)	Alnus viridis	IV
	Amelanchier ovalis	V
	Caragana arborescens	V
	Cornus florida	V
	Cornus mas	III—IV
	Corylus avellana	II—III
	Daphne mezereum	III
	Exochorda racemosa	V
	Forsythia suspensa	IV
	Chaenomeles lagenaria	IV
	Laburnum anagyroides	V
	Lonicera tatarica	V
	Mahonia aquifolium	IV—V
	Prunus spinosa	V
	Rhododendron luteum	V
	Ribes sanguineum	IV
	Ribes alpinum	IV
	Salix purpurea	IV
	Sambucus racemosa	IV—V
	Spiraea thunbergii	IV
	Viburnum carlesii	IV—V
Later-flowering from mid-May (V) to the end of June (VI)	Berberis vulgaris	V
	Colutea arborescens	VI
	Cotinus coggygria	V—VI
	Cotoneaster multiflora	VI
	Crataegus laevigata (oxyacantha)	V—VI
	Cornus sanguinea	VI
	Deutzia scabra	VI
	Ilex aquifolium	V—VI
	Ligustrum vulgare	VI
	Lonicera periclymenum	VI—VII
	Lycium halimifolium	V—IX
	Philadelphus coronarius	VI
	Rhododendron sp.	VI
	Rhus typhina	VI

Table II. (continued)

Flowering Period	Shrub	
	Rosa canina	VI
	Spiraea × vanhouttei	V—VI
	Staphylea pinnata	VI
	Syringa josikaea	VI
	Rhamnus frangula	V—VII
	Viburnum rhytidophyllum	V—VI
	Viburnum lantana	V—VI
	Viburnum opulus	VI
	Weigela florida	VI
Late-flowering July (VII) to September (IX)	Buddleia davidii	VIII—IX
	Hibiscus syriacus	VIII
	Hydrangea arborescens	VII—IX
	Rosa rugosa	VI—VIII
	Spiraea japonica	VII—VIII
	Spiraea menziesii	VII—VIII
	Symphoricarpos racemosus	VII—IX

Table III. List of Shrubs According to the Colour of Their Flowers

	Shrub	Flowering Period	Conspicuous Flower	Fragrant Flower
White Flowers	Amelanchier ovalis	V		+
	Clematis vitalba	VI—VII	+	
	Cornus florida	V	+	
	Cornus sanguinea	VI		
	Cotoneaster multiflora	VI	+	+
	Crataegus laevigata (oxyacantha)	V	+	+
	Daphne mezereum 'Album'	III	+	+
	Deutzia crenata	VI		+
	Exochorda racemosa	V	+	+
	Ilex aquifolium	V—VI		
	Hydrangea arborescens	VII—VIII	+	
	Ligustrum vulgare	VI	+	
	Lonicera xylosteum	V—VI		
	Lonicera periclymenum	VI	+	+
	Magnolia stellata	IV—V	+	+
	Mespilus germanica	V—VI	+	
	Philadelphus coronarius	VI	+	+
	Prunus spinosa	V	+	+
	Sambucus nigra	VI	+	+
	Spiraea × vanhouttei	V—VI	+	
	Staphylea pinnata	VI		+
	Syringa vulgaris	V	+	+
	Viburnum lantana	V—VI	+	
	Viburnum opulus	VI	+	+
Yellow Flowers	Berberis vulgaris	V		+
	Caragana arborescens	V		
	Colutea arborescens	VI		
	Cornus mas	III—IV	+	+
	Forsythia suspensa	IV	+	
	Laburnum anagyroides	V	+	
	Lonicera caprifolium	VI	+	+

Table III. (continued)

	Shrub	Flowering Period	Con-spicuous Flower	Fragrant Flower
	Mahonia aquifolium	III—IV	+	+
	Potentilla fruticosa	VI—VIII		
	Rhododendron luteum	V	+	
	Ribes aureum	V		+
	Rosa spinosissima	VI	+	+
	Sambucus racemosa	V		
	Sarothamnus scoparius	V—VI	+	
Pink Flowers	Chaenomeles japonica	IV	+	
	Daphne mezereum	III		+
	Lonicera tataricum	V		
	Rosa canina	V	+	+
	Spiraea salicifolia	VI	+	
	Syringa vulgaris	V	+	+
	Tamarix gallica	VI	+	
	Viburnum carlesii	IV—V	+	+
	Weigela florida	V—VI	+	+
Red Flowers	Chaenomeles lagenaria	IV	+	
	Lonicera nigra	V		
	Ribes sanguineum	IV—V	+	
	Rosa rugosa	VI—VIII	+	+
	Spiraea japonica	VI—VII	+	
	Spiraea menziesii	VII—VIII		
Violet Flowers	Hydrangea sargentiana	VII—VIII	+	
	Lycium halimifolium	V—IX		
	Syringa vulgaris	V	+	+
	Syringa josikaea	V—VI	+	+

Table IV. List of Shrubs with Ornamental Fruits

Shrub	Fruit, Colour	Months When Ripe
Berberis vulgaris	red berries	IX—XII
Cornus mas	red drupes	X—XI
Cotinus coggygria	plumose clusters of nutlets	VIII—XI
Cotoneaster species	red berries (pomes)	IX—XI
Cydonia oblonga	yellow pomes	IX—X
Crataegus laevigata (oxyacantha)	red pomes	IX—X
Euonymus europaea	orange seeds in pink capsules	IX—XII
Hippophae rhamnoides	orange drupes	IX—XII
Ilex aquifolium	red berries	IX—X
Lonicera caprifolium	red berries	VIII—X
Mahonia aquifolium	bluish berries	VIII—IX
Pyracantha coccinea	red berries (pomes)	IX—XII
Rhus typhina	hard red drupes in dense heads	IX—XII
Rosa canina	red hips	IX—XI
Rosa rugosa	red hips	VIII—XI
Sambucus racemosa	red berries	VII—VIII
Symphoricarpos albus	white berries	IX—XII
Viburnum lantana	red and black drupes	VIII—X
Viburnum opulus	red drupes	IX—XII

BIBLIOGRAPHY

Bean, W. J.: *Trees and Shrubs Hardy in the British Isles*. 8th ed. London, 1970.

Brimble, L. F. J.: *Trees in Britain*. London, 1948.

Clapham, A. R., Tutin, T. G., and Warburg, E. F.: *Flora of the British Isles*. Cambridge, 1962.

Elwes, H. J. and Henry, A. H.: *The Trees of Great Britain and Ireland*. I—VII. London, 1969.

Haworth-Booth, M.: *The Flowering Shrub Garden*. Haslemere, Surrey, 1962.

Hillier and Sons: *Manual of Trees and Shrubs*. Winchester, 1971.

Johns, C. A., Cook, E. T. and Dallimore, W.: *British Trees and Shrubs*. London, 1950.

Makins, F. K.: *The Identification of Trees and Shrubs*. London, 1948.

Osborn, A.: *Shrubs and Trees for the Garden*. London, 1945.

Rehder, A.: *Manual of Cultivated Trees and Shrubs*. New York, 1954.

Underhill, T. L.: *Heaths and Heathers*. Newton Abbot, 1971.

Zucker, Isabel: *Flowering Shrub Garden*. Haslemere, Surrey, 1962.

INDEX OF COMMON NAMES

INDEX OF LATIN NAMES